True Stories of

Bear
Attacks

Who Survived
and Why

MIKE LAPINSKI

WESTWINDS
PRESS®

In memory of Craig Dahl

Library of Congress Cataloging-in-Publication Data

Lapinski, Michael.
  True stories of bear attacks : who survived and why / by Mike Lapinski.
      p. cm.
  ISBN 978-1-55868-679-3 (softbound)
  1. Bear attacks. 2. Pepper spray. I. Title.
  QL737.C27L34 2003
  796.5'028'9—dc21

                                           2003005389

Design: Constance Bollen, cb graphics
Cartographer: Gray Mouse Graphics

WESTWINDS PRESS®
An imprint of

GRAPHIC ARTS
BOOKS®

P.O. Box 56118
Portland, OR 97238-6118
(503) 254-5591

www.graphicartsbooks.com

Contents

Range of the Black Bear

Beaufort Sea

North
Atlantic
Ocean

Labrador Sea

Gulf of
Alaska

Hudson Bay

CANADA

Pacific
Ocean

UNITED STATES

Atlantic
Ocean

Gulf of Mexico

Current

MEXICO

Range of the Grizzly Bear

Beaufort Sea

North Atlantic Ocean

Labrador Sea

Gulf of Alaska

Hudson Bay

CANADA

UNITED STATES

Atlantic Ocean

Pacific Ocean

Gulf of Mexico

MEXICO

Historic

Current

Proposed

Center for Wildlife Information, Missoula, Montana

Preface

Three days apart in the spring of 1998, two men encountered grizzly bears in the same area of Glacier National Park. One man would die; one would live. I was one of those men, so obviously I'm the one who survived—but for a few frantic seconds, I wasn't so sure it would turn out that way.

I first saw the grizzly as it walked along the shore of a lake in the Many Glacier area. The bear looked harmlessly small; they all do at a distance. The bear stopped two hundred yards from me and looked my way, then turned and walked away from me on a diagonal with a stiff-legged gait.

I waited until the bear moved out of sight, and then I entered a relatively open five-acre grove of aspens whose fresh lime-green leaves had recently burst forth. Halfway through the grove, I abruptly halted amidst a dense growth of thigh-high ferns. The hair raised on the back of my neck and a feeling of dread slowly spread over me. There was a mile of open shoreline and grass beyond the aspens, but the bear was nowhere in sight. The only other place the bear could be was in the aspen grove—and I was standing in the middle of it.

My mind flashed back to a story I'd read about two bear researchers who were tracking a grizzly, who began laying ambushes for them by circling ahead and flattening himself behind logs. Twenty yards ahead of me lay a large spruce log. I strained to spot a tuft of grizzled fur, a movement—anything that would show me that the bear was indeed there. And then the wind shifted, bringing to my nostrils the faint odor of putrid flesh, probably from an elk that the bear had killed earlier. I had no doubt the grizzly was lying behind that log, waiting.

The hysterical impulse to turn and run was overpowering, but my mind screamed for me to stay calm because I was still in control. Though I carried no gun, I was not defenseless. I slowly removed the large can of bear pepper spray from my hip holster and released the safety. Twice before, I'd used bear spray to thwart attacks by black bears, and I knew from the experiences of many people that it would stop even a grizzly.

I backed up one nudging step at a time until I reached the edge of the grove. I hurried away, hiking in a wide circle over a series of small cliffs, and eventually made it back to my vehicle, tired and shaken, but pleased that the bear pepper spray had once again kept me not only safe but also in control of my mental and physical actions.

Twenty miles away and three days later, Craig Dahl, a twenty-six-year-old park employee, went for a day hike in the Two Medicine Lake area. When he didn't show up for work the next morning, a search party was sent out.

Searchers spotted his tracks in a receding snowfield and found where he'd begun running downhill. Following his tracks, they soon came upon a chilling discovery—galloping grizzly tracks that converged upon human footprints. It was impossible to tell whether Craig Dahl had run after spotting the big sow and her two half-grown cubs or if he'd run after the bear charged. His partially consumed body was found a short distance away. Of course, the sow and her cubs also paid for their part in the tragedy. They were all shot.

Two men encounter surly grizzly bears. One man dies and one lives. Craig Dahl turned and ran—an action likely to trigger a predatory response in a bear. But I had also erred. I entered that aspen grove knowing that a bear was somewhere ahead. Big mistake. And that stiff-legged posture as the grizzly walked away was a sure sign of agitation in the bear. I hadn't been alert to these danger signs at the time, but as I pondered the two encounters, with their diverging results, I realized that I too had violated the code of proper conduct with bears.

It's like that in bear country. You can do a lot of things that, in retrospect, are mistakes. Like hiking along a brushy trail. No bear, no problem. Big bear, big problem. As part of my work in teaching people how to defend against bear attacks, I spend much of my time roaming the habitat of large predators. And I've come to realize that sooner or later it happens to everyone: through no conscious fault of your own, you find yourself in a potentially dangerous situation.

When that happens, all the cute statistics—like the one about how you are 380 times more likely to die from a bee sting than from a bear bite—vaporize in the twenty yards that separate you from an animal twice as powerful pound for pound as any person and capable of tearing out huge chunks of your flesh with its powerful jaws.

Though I was terrified that day in Glacier, I didn't run from the lurking grizzly because I still felt in control. A twelve-ounce can of bear pepper spray gave me the confidence to think clearly in a very dangerous situation. And even if the bear had charged, a mauling was not a foregone conclusion. I've successfully sprayed two bears and a mountain lion and seen the awesome effects of airborne red-hot pepper.

As I write this preface, I'm staring at a clipping fresh out of the newspaper about a bear mauling. The incident occurred at Two Medicine Lake near the place where Craig Dahl died. A twenty-four-year-old man was stalked and chased around a tree by a black bear several times before being mauled—plenty of time to give the marauding bruin a snootful of pepper and send it on its way with a good dose of aversive conditioning toward humans. But the man wasn't carrying bear pepper spray, and the incident ended tragically. Not so much for the man—he was treated at the hospital and released—but for the bear: it was given a permanent dose of aversive conditioning when it was shot and killed by park rangers.

The purpose of this book is to encourage travelers in bear country to carry bear pepper spray—not only for their own welfare but also for the welfare of the bear, because it's the bruin that usually ends up dead if there's trouble. I interviewed dozens of people who were attacked by bears, and I'll relate in detail how bear pepper spray, properly used, stopped both black bears and grizzly bears, saving these folks from horrible maulings, even death.

I also interviewed a few people who used bear spray with only limited success, and these incidents will be dissected to glean some understanding of what went wrong. And for those who would choose the use of a gun over bear spray, there will be several chilling accounts of men and women who were mauled by bears despite the fact that the people carried high-powered rifles.

Wisdom is better than strength: the best way to escape a bear attack is to know how to avoid situations that can lead to a confrontation. Chapters explaining bear behavior and aggression will arm you with the wisdom to avoid most dangerous circumstances. If the unforeseen occurs, that canister of bear spray on your hip will do the rest.

I wish I didn't have to write this preface about a dead man. I wish I'd met Craig Dahl that spring, showed him my bear spray, and offered him the spare can I always carry. But it's too late for Craig Dahl. It's not too late for you.

Acknowledgments

I could never have written this book without the help and encouragement of numerous individuals and organizations. After I mentioned to Mark Matheny, whose UDAP company manufactures bear-deterrent pepper spray, that I was thinking of writing a book about bears and about use of such sprays, Mark hounded me until I began working on it, then gave me free access to all information he possessed. I also benefited from the help of another bear spray manufacturer, Counter Assault, whose staff furnished me with much information about the birth and development of the industry. Indeed, it was an honor to interview company founder Bill Pounds, whose tenacity and ingenuity led to his discovery of the value of red pepper as a bear deterrent.

Much of my information came from hours of poring through newspaper files until I found a bear-attack story, then interviewing the victims. At the office of the *Hungry Horse News* in Columbia Falls, Montana, editor Chris Petersen gave me access to more than a decade of newspaper archives, from which many of the stories in this book originated. The *Missoulian* newspaper in Missoula, Montana, provided generous help in seeking out vital bear incidents.

And then there's Chuck Bartlebaugh, director of the Center for Wildlife Information, in Missoula. Chuck fights the battle for wise stewardship of all wild animals, but especially bears, with a subtle ferocity. He acted as my mentor—intermittently encouraging, cajoling, correcting me—as I groped through much of the political haze surrounding bear policy and federal standards for bear spray. In this world where so much, even bear conservation, is money-driven, Chuck remains true to the cause of educating the public about bear safety.

Other recognized bear experts who shared their expertise with me include Jay Gore, Barry Gilbert, Stephen Herrero, Chuck Jonkel, and Tim Manley. I am truly humbled that men of such stature and reputation would take time out from their busy schedules to entertain my questions.

In my writing, I was helped and inspired by a number of important books, including *Mark of the Grizzly,* by Scott McMillion, which showed that a bear book can also display literary excellence, and Doug Peacock's masterpiece, *Grizzly Years,* a book with a heart and soul. For pure expertise and scientific analysis, you can't beat Stephen Herrero's *Bear Attacks: Their Causes and Avoidance.* James Gary Sheldon's *Bear Attacks: The Deadly Truth* is an excellent work by a man who brings great insight to the aggressive tendencies of bears. Brad Garfield's *Bear vs. Man* is another good book for learning why bears act the way they do. And I certainly can't forget *Alaska Bear Tales* by Larry Kaniut with its astonishing narratives of hair-raising bear encounters.

Most importantly, I thank the many people who survived bear attacks and shared their stories with me. Through their openness and courage, this book was made possible.

CHAPTER 1

Bear Troubles

A few years ago a spokesman for the Humane Society contacted Glacier National Park officials and asked if they knew of a grizzly bear whose life story might serve as the basis for an uplifting children's book. An official suggested a sow grizzly known as Chocolate Legs as a good candidate to help youngsters understand bears.

Born in the Many Glacier area of the park in 1982, the female cub had been abandoned by her mother and was found wandering in a campground. She was relocated, and biologists hoped that by some miracle she might survive the winter. In a rare occurrence, the yearling was adopted the next spring by another sow grizzly and survived her perilous early years.

She matured into a beautiful bear with a light upper body and dark brown legs. Park rangers began calling her Chocolate Legs. Though she had a few problems with humans, such as frequenting a campground and making a nuisance of herself, she had apparently been the closest thing to a good bear that you could expect to find.

The story of Chocolate Legs appeared in a colorfully illustrated, thirty-two-page children's book that told of a good and gentle bear, tolerant of humans, who overcame great adversity and thrived. So heartwarming was the story that it almost made you forget that Chocolate was a wild grizzly bear. The book—*Chocolate, A Glacier Grizzly*—was published in April 1998.

One month later, Chocolate Legs killed and ate Craig Dahl. In turn, she and her two cubs were shot to death.

Here's the problem with trying to characterize the behavior of bears: just when you think you've got them all figured out, they do the most unpredictable things. Sometimes their antics are cute, like playfully sliding down a snowfield over and over; or worrisome, like following closely behind a group of hikers; or frightening, like rushing in a sudden bluff charge that leaves a hiker trembling with fear.

This problem with bear behavior is not so much a bruin problem as it is a human one. People who respect and love the bear, having seen how human prejudice and ignorance have led to wholesale slaughter of the animal, often lay humanistic labels on bears, like the term *good bear*. A bear whose actions fall in line with human expectations of proper behavior is labeled a good bear.

You can't blame sympathetic bear biologists for hastily placing that label on a bear, because the alternative is to label it a problem bear. That dreadful moniker equates to a death sentence when the bear is eventually killed for any of a number of capital offenses, such as eating birdseed or dog food foolishly left out at a rural residence or tearing apart a tent where smelly food was stored.

Oftentimes the difference between a good bear and a problem

bear lies more in the realm of chance and opportunity than in any conditioned behavior. As much as we'd like to believe that a bear can eventually learn right from wrong, a bear can neither reason nor rationalize. It is a big, powerful animal that reacts instinctively, and just when you start thinking you've got a bear figured out, you're due for a traumatic attitude adjustment.

This happened to my friend Marvin Moe, a nail-tough logger from Libby, Montana, who has seen his share of grizzlies while spending most of his life in the vast mountains surrounding that isolated logging town forty miles south of the Canadian border. Marvin has thrown rocks at grizzlies to get them out of camp, blown the horn on his logging truck to get them off the road, and generally shrugged off all the hype about the dangers they pose.

That is until the spring day he was driving his pickup truck down a dirt road north of Libby and spotted a sow grizzly with two cubs feeding on the succulent new grass shoots sprouting next to the road. Marvin pulled off the road and came around to the passenger's side of the pickup and leaned against the hood with arms folded and legs crossed, enjoying the scene, as he'd done many times before.

The sow raised her head and eyed him for a few seconds, then returned to feeding about forty yards away. The bear suddenly turned toward Marvin and bounced stiff-legged, woofing. Startled, Marvin decided it was time to get back in the pickup. He hurried around the front, but when he glanced back, he was shocked to see the sow in full charge just twenty yards away. Realizing he wouldn't make it to the pickup door in time, he dove under the vehicle.

"There I was, lying on my back under that pickup, watching the bear's legs pace back and forth," Marvin told me. "She peeked underneath and started snapping her jaws and trying to hook me out from under it. A couple times her claws just about had me.

"I scooted to the other side, but she came around and tried to crawl underneath after me. Thank God she was big and had that hump. She couldn't quite fit underneath, but that just seemed to make her madder. For almost five minutes she circled that pickup, taking swipes at me. Finally, she walked away and took her cubs into the woods."

Marvin folded his arms and spoke adamantly. "No more for me. That bear made a believer out of me. I'm staying away from grizzlies from now on."

■ ■ ■

While grizzlies have a well-deserved reputation for being unpredictable and aggressive, the black bear has a reputation for being timid. However, it is a fact that the majority of property damage and personal injury, including deaths, is attributable to the black bear. In the summer of 1999, five maulings plus two deaths—that of a teacher, in Great Smoky Mountains National Park, and of one of Canada's top women biathletes, while running on a training course near the city of Quebec—were caused by black bears. During that same period, no grizzly attacks were recorded in the United States or Canada.

During the 1984–1992 period throughout British Columbia, twenty-five people were injured and five were killed by black bears. During that same time, four people were injured and one person was killed by grizzlies. These disparities can partly be accounted for by the fact there are far more black bears than grizzlies—but they still show that you don't dare take black bears for granted.

For some reason as yet unknown, black bears tend to be more predatory than grizzlies toward humans; most grizzly attacks result when a bear is surprised at close range. And unlike the furious rush of a grizzly, a black bear attack—while rare—tends to be a progressive thing, with the bear often running away, then coming back to assess a human's vulnerability. This may be a long, drawn-out process while a black bear follows a hiker until it has built up its courage to attack.

George Regan is a man who has encountered several black bears in the wild, and all of them ran away—except for one. A few years ago while he was examining a stand of trees in western Montana for the timber harvest, George surprised a 150-pound black bear. The bear started to run off but stopped sixty yards away. Since the bear was smallish and was just sitting there, George was not concerned. Eventually the bear slowly walked off.

George continued measuring trees and writing notes in his field book. A twig snapped behind him, and he turned to find the bear forty yards away. He yelled and stamped his feet, and the bear retreated, but it soon returned and began following him, moving ever closer until it was just fifteen yards away. The bear ignored sticks and rocks thrown at it and began posturing aggressively, turning sideways and lolling its head back and forth. Then it began gnashing its teeth and making short, stiff-legged bluff charges. Fortunately, George wasn't far from his vehicle and he slowly retreated to it, never turning his back on the bear, before the animal could work up the courage to attack.

"I've never been afraid of black bears," George told me. "I thought of them as nothing more than big, black dogs, but I have to admit that bear had me scared, especially when I realized I had nothing to stop it from attacking me. I felt so vulnerable." I gave

George a can of bear pepper spray, and he faithfully carries it whenever he enters the woods.

■ ■ ■

A black bear sow with cubs has the potential to be every bit as dangerous as a grizzly. Idaho resident David Rust related that he was hiking along an open ridge one summer day, mapping a route to build a road into a small parcel of land he had purchased near the Idaho–Montana border. He entered a clearing and spotted a black bear sow with two cubs.

At that point Dave wasn't worried. He'd encountered scores of bears in the woods and never had a problem. Besides, he felt the hundred and fifty yards that separated man from bear gave the sow plenty of room to avoid feeling threatened. As he continued walking, the sow suddenly looked over and stood on her hind feet. Just to make sure the sow realized he was a human, Dave waved his arms and yelled. The sow dropped down and came running.

Concerned that the bear still didn't realize he was a human, he decided to climb a tree, just in case. He'd climbed about sixteen feet up a red fir tree by the time the sow arrived. The bear stood on her hind feet and placed her paws on the trunk of the tree. As the bear stared up at him, Dave thought: *Good, she sees me and knows I'm a human. Now she'll leave.*

Instead, the sow began climbing the tree, gnashing her teeth as she advanced. Dave yelled and kicked at the bear. The sow stopped and stared up at him as he threw limbs at it. The loud yelling seemed to unnerve her. Good thing, too, because the bear's head was only a few feet from his boots. Finally, the sow scrambled down the tree and loped off toward her cubs.

"That experience totally changed the way I think about black bears," Dave told me.

Stan Anderson can attest to the power of a black bear, and to the damage its claws and jaws can inflict. Stan, a retired schoolteacher, likes to stay fit by hiking close to his beautiful mountain home near the small town of Eureka in northwest Montana. One morning Stan chose to hike a secluded grassy road lined with stately ponderosa pine and Douglas fir trees.

He kept his chocolate Labrador, Ole, at his side, because when Ole wanders off, he has a knack for getting in trouble and bringing it back to Stan. A few weeks earlier, Stan had visited a creek to do some fishing, and the irrepressible Ole wandered up the stream. Suddenly, Stan heard a furious splashing upstream, and he looked up to see his terrified dog lunging down the middle of the creek with a cow moose in close pursuit. To Stan's horror, Ole ran straight to him. Stan hid behind a bush and Ole dove right between his master's legs. The infuriated moose ran up to the bush, then stuck her big nose right through the shrub. Man and moose eyed each other from a distance of about three feet, then the moose ran off.

Later, Stan laughed as he related the incident to me. "When they handed out the fight in dogs, they overlooked my Ole. He's afraid of his own shadow. When he sees a moth, he backs up." Fortunately, Stan was wrong about his dog.

That fateful morning, Stan had hiked about a mile along the road when he saw a small black bear cub scoot across the lane sixty yards in front of him. He grabbed his dog's collar and muttered, "Ole, we'd better clear out of here." He walked briskly to put distance between himself and the bear.

"I'd gone about a hundred yards when I heard scrambling behind me and turned to see the sow coming like an express train," Stan recalled. "She covered that distance in about three seconds. She never slowed down, just hauled back and swatted my face."

As the sow grabbed for the fallen man's head, Ole leaped forward and began tearing at the bear's rump, which eventually unnerved the bruin and drove her back toward her cub. Bleeding profusely from his face wounds, Stan gingerly took a flopping piece of cheek that had been torn loose by the bear and laid it back against his face.

He regained his feet and started walking away at a swift pace, but when he looked back, he was horrified to see the sow charging at him again. The bear barreled into him, sending him sprawling.

"She started chewing on my arm pretty good," Stan said, "then she moved up to my shoulder. I thought for sure I was dead."

Suddenly the bear bawled and jerked backward. Ole was furiously biting the bear's rump. The unnerved bear took a swat at the dog, then galloped back to her cub.

Stan stumbled to his feet. Blood poured down his face and into his eyes, making it difficult to see where he was going as he stumbled the mile back to his old car. Ole jumped into his usual place in the backseat and Stan drove off for help.

As he drove down the road, the blood in his eyes made driving difficult. Then shock set in, and he struggled to remain conscious. But just when he thought he might pass out, Ole scrambled into the passenger's front seat and began whimpering and licking at his master's face. Stan stayed conscious long enough to get to a farmhouse three miles down the road, and from there an ambulance rushed him to a hospital.

This incident and the others related in this chapter graphically illustrate the unpredictability of both grizzly and black bears as it pertains to human expectations of proper bear behavior. While it may never be possible to fully predict a bear's actions, studies by bear biologists are helping us to better understand bear behavior. And the closer we come to understanding the bear, the closer we come to predicting its actions.

CHAPTER 2

Why Bears Attack

B lack and grizzly bears may look somewhat similar, but their personalities and instincts vary greatly, with the black bear being much more timid than the grizzly. That's because the bigger, more powerful and tenacious grizzly looks upon its smaller cousin as fair game. If a black bear encounters a grizzly, the tendency of the black bear is to run away. But the grizzly is prone to aggressively confront the black bear, oftentimes running it down and killing it as prey.

Such an encounter was observed by a photographer I met in Yellowstone National Park. The man watched through binoculars as a black bear fed on a calf elk carcass near Slough Creek in the Lamar Valley. A grizzly bear emerged from the timber, having caught the scent of the blood and gore. The grizzly made a careful stalk and, in a sudden rush, pounced on the black bear and quickly killed it. The grizzly then spent several days contentedly feeding on both the elk and black bear.

As a result of its tenuous status two links down on the food chain (below humans and grizzlies), the instinctive reaction of a black bear is to run when it encounters a person. However, that basic reaction can change, especially if the bear has lost its instinctive fear of people. Then it may ignore the human, and in rare instances even work up the courage for a predatory attack.

However, black bear attacks and aggressive behavior toward humans are rare. Statistics show that black bears inflict more property damage and injury to humans than grizzlies do, but that's mainly because there are mega-times more black bears than grizzlies in the Lower 48 states. Estimates put grizzly numbers at about thirteen hundred, while black bears have increased to almost a million. Black bears are found in all but seven states (Delaware, Hawaii, Illinois, Indiana, Iowa, Kansas, and Nebraska), often living near areas inhabited by humans.

Any encounter with a black bear carries the potential for a confrontation, and caution should always be used around any bear. But the fact remains that the vast majority of black bears instinctively flee when they become aware of a human's presence.

On the other hand, grizzly behavior, as it pertains to humans, is far more complex, and anyone who ventures into bear country should learn how grizzlies act, and react, to humans. Grizzlies have behavioral tendencies that are primal, especially when it comes to aggression, and a look at history explains why. The grizzly bear, evolving about thirteen thousand years ago in the Pleistocene epoch, was not at the top of the food chain. Life among a host of large predators, such as the cave bear and saber-toothed tiger, was harsh, and the grizzly bear developed a defensive-aggressive personality that is its trademark today. Rather than fall prey to a faster, equally lethal large predator, the grizzly developed the trait of confronting danger with furious bluff charges, sometimes including attacks, to render the other animal defenseless.

This is the instinctive reaction that leads to most grizzly attacks. When encountered at close range, a grizzly's defensive-aggressive mechanism is triggered, which may lead to a bluff charge that leaves a human terrified. In its agitated state a grizzly may go one step further by swatting, biting, or shaking a human. To the bear, this is an inconsequential neutralizing action that may last mere seconds.

Unfortunately, the tremendous power of a grizzly, coupled with its massive ripping teeth and four-inch-long claws, can tear apart a frail human body in seconds. A grizzly attack near Banff, Alberta, is a sobering example. The bear briefly attacked a fisherman, then moved off. When searchers arrived at the attack site, they found a piece of the man's lower jawbone containing nine teeth. A short distance away they found the man's nose and an ear, before finding the victim, who died the next day.

The good news is that even the mighty grizzly bear harbors an instinctive fear of humans. Way back in that same Pleistocene epoch, the bear also encountered a relatively frail creature who walked upright and carried sharp sticks that were lethal. From thousands of years of hard lessons learned, it's in a bear's genes to flee from a human if given the opportunity.

When confronted with a situation in which the grizzly feels threatened, a bear may exhibit defensive-aggressive posturing, such as woofing and popping its teeth, bluff-charging, or bouncing stiff-legged. These aggressive posturings are intended to remove the threat, because a bear has no way of knowing that the petite grandmotherly woman standing in the trail thirty yards away means it no harm.

There are four principal situations that have the potential to trigger a bear attack. These are the situations to learn about and to avoid. The four scenarios involve a bear that has been startled, a bear that is guarding its food cache, a bear that is defending its young, and a predatory bear.

■ ■ ■

Dangerous situation number one has as its focus a startled bear. Ninety percent of all grizzly attacks occur when a human stumbles upon a bear. No situation triggers a bear's defensive-aggressive reaction more quickly than the sudden appearance of a human within fifty yards. If you can avoid startling a bear, you'll prevent most trouble in bear country.

Unfortunately it's not as easy as it sounds. The alpine grizzly habitat of Glacier National Park affords plenty of sight distance for bear and human to avoid a confrontation, yet several attacks occur there each year. That's because trails occasionally pass through dense forest or along brushy sidehills or streams where solitary bears like to bed down during the heat of the day and where they feed because vegetation is more succulent. Upon entering one of these closed-in areas, a smart hiker yells or sings—anything to alert a bear of his or her presence before the bear is faced with a fight-or-flight situation.

A problem with most hikers is that they are too shy about making noise. A self-conscious monotone will usually fail to alert a bear of your approach. Bear researcher Stephen Herrero said that bears have been unaware of his presence even though he spoke in a conversational tone just 150 feet away. You have to yell to get a bear's attention, especially if you're hiking along a noisy mountain stream.

For years, people have used large bear bells, but research now seems to indicate that bears often ignore their steady musical jingle.

Though he emphasizes that it's too early to draw definitive conclusions, Tom Smith of the U.S. Geological Survey's Alaska Science Center tested a group of brown bears and found that they seemed to pay the bells no mind at all. Along the coast in Katmai National Park, Smith hid near a well-traveled bear path. Whenever a bear passed by, Smith pulled on a fishing line attached to a string of bells that were tied to an alder bush alongside the trail. Not one bear looked in the direction of the noise or even perked up its ears.

Smith said he first tinkled the bells lightly. Then he yanked on the line, making a loud jangling noise "almost as loud as a fire alarm." Fifteen groups of one or more bears walked past. Not one flinched.

Smith then tried snapping a pencil to simulate the sound of a twig breaking. The bears immediately turned and looked toward his hiding place in a blind about 150 feet away. A loud huff, mimicking the sound of another bear, also got the bears' attention.

Smith, in summarizing his little experiment, said, "This doesn't mean that bear bells don't work. It just means that bears didn't respond the way we thought." Smith speculated that perhaps bears tune out noises such as tinkling bells or droning human voices because they sound too much like nonthreatening background sounds such as a rushing stream, birds chirping, or insects buzzing.

I've discovered one noise that works very well to alert bears: just bark like a dog. A friend of mine, Larry Bennet, who used hounds to chase mountain lions and black bears in Idaho, told me that although lions or bears can easily kill a dog, they run up trees because the loud baying and barking bother them. I've barked at bears from a distance, and this sound, even from a weak human mouth, instantly alerts the bears and sends them in the opposite direction.

I have noticed another dangerous tendency among hikers in closed-in grizzly habitat: they hike too fast, often at five miles per hour. A swiftly moving hiker runs the risk of striding into a bear's path before the bruin is given a chance to flee. An experienced hiker slows down when hiking through dense cover and around corners, making plenty of loud, staccato noise to give bears ample opportunity to depart.

If you find yourself on a dense, brushy stretch of trail containing fresh bear scat or tracks, it may be best to look for an open area that you can detour through in order to avoid surprising a bear. If that's not possible, consider backing off and choosing another trail— or cut your hike short rather than risk a sudden encounter.

■ ■ ■

Dangerous situation number two involves a bear that is protecting its food. Life is hard in bear country. The massive muscle structure of a bear, plus the fact that it needs to store up an ample reserve of fat to make it through hibernation, creates a gluttonous drive for food. But grass and a few grubs barely provide enough day-to-day sustenance. Being omnivorous, a bear is always on the lookout for a large supply of protein, such as carrion, the decaying bodies of dead animals.

However, a bear is not above "creating" carrion by killing large animals such as elk, moose, or buffalo. Researchers tracking a radio-collared grizzly in Yellowstone National Park related how the big bear would lie behind logs or overturned root wads next to game trails and kill any elk passing by.

When a protein-starved bear, be it a black or grizzly, finds or kills a big animal, it gorges on it, then covers the rest with dirt and forest debris to hide it from other scavengers or birds. Being more timid by nature, a black bear may retreat when disturbed at a carcass. However, any grizzly is very dangerous when disturbed at its food cache.

Howard Copenhaver, an outfitter in Montana's Bob Marshall Wilderness, once stumbled upon a large boar (male) grizzly guarding its cache. Howard barely made it up a skinny lodgepole pine tree ahead of the enraged bear. Howard feared that his brother would hike over the ridge at any moment and fall prey to the bear, so he waited until the animal returned to feed on the carcass, then he slid down the tree and hit the ground running. The bear was after him in a heartbeat. Howard shinnied up a second tree, spurred on by the loud snapping of the bear's jaws just inches from his boots, but the risky move did put him twenty yards farther from the carcass.

Twice more, Howard and the bear played their deadly game until Howard was in a tree about a hundred yards from the bear's cache. He was finally able to climb down and slip away without the bear snapping at his heels. Good thing, too, because he met his brother a short time later, hiking up the trail.

Howard was fortunate. Due to his wiry build and tree-climbing ability, he lived to tell his story. Sadly, for Marcie Trent and her son, Larry Waldron, someone else was left with the dreadful chore of piecing together what happened when they stumbled upon a grizzly guarding its food cache in Alaska's Chugach State Park.

That morning in the summer of 1995, with Larry in the lead and Marcie back a few hundred yards with her fourteen-year-old grandson, they jogged up a trail toward a dense alder thicket. Inside the thicket, a grizzly bear was guarding the carcass of a moose that it had killed. Larry was attacked first. The bear delivered horrific injuries, leaving him dead about thirty yards below the trail. As

Marcie and her grandson approached the moose carcass, the bear rushed them from the thicket and quickly killed Marcie. Her grandson escaped by sliding down the steep hillside through the alder brush while the bear was attacking Marcie.

A hiker who spots a bear pacing back and forth in a small area should back away and not even skirt the area because the bear may have cubs up a tree or a food cache nearby. If you stumble upon an area in the forest that has been scraped down to the dirt, with a large pile of forest debris nearby, it's probably a food cache. The bear will be somewhere nearby, and you should quietly retreat.

Hunters in grizzly country who kill a game animal and then leave the carcass to go for help in packing it out should approach the carcass with great care when they return. There are tragic stories of hunters who hurried back to claim their game animal, only to be confronted by a grizzly that had moved in and claimed the carcass. If there is any sign of a disturbance at the kill site, such as a disturbed carcass, or debris piled on top of it, leave the area at once to avoid a confrontation. Give the carcass to the bear.

There is another, more disturbing, aspect to this tendency of an opportunistic grizzly to move in and claim a hunter's game animal. It appears that in late fall some bears will actually move toward the location of rifle shots, having learned that these sudden noises usually produce the protein-rich food they badly need before going into hibernation.

Eric Burge was hunting in Gallatin Canyon north of Yellowstone National Park one November when he heard two rifle shots. A few seconds later he heard a commotion coming from a stand of trees fifty yards away. He turned in time to see a sow grizzly and two large cubs lope out of the trees, obviously excited and looking in the direction of the shots.

"There's no doubt in my mind," Eric said, "that those bears were responding to the sound of those two shots. You could see it in their eyes. They stopped in front of me, pacing back and forth, but their eyes weren't on the terrain in front of them. They were looking off into the distance, trying to pinpoint the location of those shots. The sow finally took off toward a ridge where I had guessed the shots came from, and her cubs hurried after her."

Dave Moody of the Wyoming Game and Fish Department says that grizzlies are intelligent opportunists. "When they find a fresh gut pile or carcass hanging in the trees after a few gunshots resounded from that area, the next time they hear shots they're going to move toward those shots."

■ ■ ■

Dangerous situation number three arises with a bear that is defending its young. A leading cause of mortality among sub-adult grizzly bears is bigger bears. A large boar grizzly will pounce upon any cub to kill and eat it. For that reason, a sow grizzly is one of the most ferocious and dangerous animals to stumble upon in bear country. You may be a seventy-year-old grandmother with nothing but love in your heart for all the animals in the woods, but the sow grizzly you encounter does not know that. She looks upon all intruders, human or beast, as potential sources of harm to her cubs, and she will aggressively defend them to the death.

So what happens when a human unwittingly winds up in circumstances that involve three of the four dangerous situations that can lead to a bear attack—by startling a grizzly with cubs protecting her food cache? Big trouble, as Mark Matheny of Bozeman, Montana, quickly learned one sunny autumn afternoon.

Mark and his bowhunting partner, Fred Bahnson, were hiking along a ridge trail in southwestern Montana's Gallatin National Forest about forty miles north of Yellowstone National Park. Mark had bagged a dandy mule deer buck that morning, and the men were in good spirits as they hiked at a brisk pace toward the trailhead two miles away.

Mark, in the lead, said the first indication of trouble came when three crows suddenly flapped skyward from behind a blown-down tree. Unknown to him, a sow grizzly and her two cubs were feeding there on a dead cow elk. Mark heard a *woof* from behind the tree, and the huge grizzly exploded toward him, followed by the cubs. Mark had time to yell a terse warning back to his partner: "Fred, it's a bear! Get your spray!"

Mark threw up his bow for protection, but the onrushing sow slapped it out of his hands and hammered him to the ground. The enraged animal bit his arms, face, and head, and shook him violently.

Fred grabbed a small can of bear pepper spray from his backpack and advanced, yelling, toward the bear. The sow turned and slapped the can of bear spray from Fred's hands, then knocked him down and bit him on the back and arms before returning to again maul Mark.

Stunned and bleeding, Fred struggled to his feet, grabbed the can of bear spray, and came at the bear again. He sprayed the bear from a distance of five feet. The bear bawled, jerked her head backward, then galloped away with her cubs trailing behind. Though both men were bleeding from multiple tear wounds, they were able to help each other out of the forest.

That day changed Mark Matheny's life forever. The courage of a friend, and a small can of bear pepper spray, had saved him. With military zeal, the ex-marine went about developing an improved

pepper spray for stopping grizzly bears. He is now the owner of
UDAP (Universal Defense Alternative Products), a leading manufacturer of bear-deterrent pepper spray. Mark is a vocal proponent
of bear pepper spray as an alternative to shooting bears that show
aggression.

■ ■ ■

Dangerous situation number four involves a predatory bear. A
deadly incident in July 2000 in Alaska illustrates this threat. George
Tullos, a forty-one-year-old resident of Ketchikan, went to sleep in
the Run Amuck Campground about seventy-five miles northeast of
town. He had little cause to fear bears, because the fishing run was
on and the bears were blissfully gorging on salmon. Besides, these
were bears so conditioned to humans that the U.S.D.A. Forest
Service maintained a bear-viewing site about three miles away, where
people could watch the big brown bears wander by as close as
twenty yards away without showing any signs of aggression. These
were coastal grizzlies—usually referred to in Alaska as brown bears
to differentiate them from the smaller inland grizzlies, though they
are the same species.

But that night the campground had a rare visitor—a predatory
brown bear. The next morning George Tullos's body was found,
ravaged and partially consumed. The 300-pound male bear was
quickly located and shot.

Authorities said the bear had appeared in the area ten days earlier
and had shown aggressive tendencies, such as chasing a group of
campers away from their packs and then pawing through the packs
for food. The bear had been seen scavenging for food at the local
dump, but an autopsy on the bear showed that his diet also included

the more usual grass and berries. Also found in the stomach was human flesh.

"We don't see many bears around like this, thank goodness," said Paul Larkin, operator of the bear-viewing site. "This was a bear who was an opportunist that took advantage of what he could find."

It is a chilling fact that a small percentage of both black and grizzly bears look upon humans as food. In the past, some well-intentioned people feared that any suggestion that a bear might view humans as prey would send folks scurrying for their guns to shoot any bear. So they cultivated the philosophy that there were no bad bears—only bad people.

Thus any bear attack would be dissected until some fragment of evidence was discovered to prove that the bear had been artificially conditioned (habituated) to lose its fear of people. This certainly was true in many of the maulings involving bears that had become accustomed to eating human's food from garbage dumps and had lost their instinctive fear of humans.

Bear biologist Stephen Herrero, whose book *Bear Attacks: Their Causes and Avoidance* is the bible for understanding bear aggression, found that most attacks came from habituated bears. However, Herrero's region of research was Canada's Banff National Park, where bears and humans have a history of dangerous interaction. Bear expert Gary Shelton, who teaches bear-encounter survival courses to Canadian government and timber company employees, pointed out that 75 percent of all attacks in British Columbia are by bears who have had little or no human contact.

Away from the garbage dumps and crowded campgrounds, bears have stalked and killed humans for no discernible reason other than that they consider them as prey. But whether a bear has become human-habituated or not is a moot point when that bear looks upon a human as its potential food. Travelers in bear country need to recognize the danger, however small, that a black or grizzly bear may approach them as a predator—not out of curiosity or as a defensive-aggressive reaction, but to kill them for food. In this situation, a bear will sneak forward, often from behind or hidden by cover. A traveler should keep an eye out behind and to the side for a bear that may be in a predatory mode. There will be no bluff charges; any charge by this bear will be only too real.

All this talk about predatory bears and enraged sows bursting out of the forest is enough to scare the casual hiker out of the woods. It shouldn't. I average about fifty hours in the woods for every bear sighting. You're not in mortal danger the second you step into bear country. Travelers who try their best to avoid startling a bear, and who leave an area immediately after becoming aware of a bear, should encounter few problems.

■ ■ ■

What should you do if, through no fault of your own, you find yourself face-to-face with an aggressive bear? Essentially, you have three choices: submit, escape, or defend yourself.

Before a charging bear gets to you, you can drop to the ground in a submissive position, lying belly down to protect vital organs, with hands clasped over the back of your neck. Or you can curl on your side into a fetal position, with knees tucked under your chin.

A few lucky people who tried the tactic of submission have avoided injury when a charging bear simply sniffed them and left. But the usual scenario has the bear cuff and bite the victim a few times before leaving. One woman who was charged by a grizzly dropped onto her belly. The bear merely sniffed her, then started to leave, but as an afterthought turned back and bit her once on a buttock, removing a large portion of it.

If an oncoming grizzly is some distance away, you can try to escape by climbing a tree. Grizzlies don't usually climb trees. However, Gary Shelton has recorded several instances in which threatened travelers climbed trees, only to have the grizzly follow up in pursuit.

I once had a ringside seat to such a spectacle. While working for a video company, I coproduced and filmed much of the video titled *Bear Attacks*. To illustrate the technique of climbing a tree to escape a bear attack, we had a man walk up to a trained grizzly along a trail and then climb a nearby tree. The man scooted up the tree in a matter of seconds while the bear trotted forward. To our surprise, the grizzly easily followed him up the tree by hooking its paws over the branches.

Wade Sjodin and Louie Van Grootel, workers in the Canadian woods, were once charged by a grizzly. Though they carried pepper spray, they decided to escape by climbing into trees, and in the process the spray was left in their vests on the ground. Louie had difficulty climbing his tree, and the bear severely mauled him while Wade climbed forty feet up another tree. The bear then turned to Wade. The grizzly lunged up Wade's tree, and in four seconds was at his feet. The bear hung on with one paw and bit into Wade's thigh, pulling downward furiously to dislodge him, tearing skin and flesh.

With his free leg, Wade kicked the bear hard in the face, but the grizzly latched onto the heel of the boot, released its grip on the tree, and used its entire three-hundred-pound weight to jerk downward. This tremendous force tore Wade's arms from the tree, and he crashed to the ground alongside the bear.

Both man and bear lay stunned for a few seconds. Then Wade struggled to his feet and jumped behind the tree as the bear lunged at him. Wade's vest was at the base of the tree, and he grabbed the can of bear pepper spray as the bear chased him. He sprayed the bear from a distance of a few feet, and the grizzly instantly ran off, wiping its face with its paws.

Wade climbed the tree again—but watched in horror as the bear returned and once more climbed up after him. He sprayed it again, and the bear fell from the tree and stumbled off. Though both men were seriously injured, they survived the attack.

The third response to a bear attack is to defend yourself. Guns are an option, but don't be misled into thinking that a gun will ensure your protection from a mauling when a bear attacks. The stories in Chapter 6 are a startling reminder of this fact. In any case, firearms are illegal in national parks, where most grizzlies are found in the Lower 48 states, and Canada has restrictions on U.S. citizens carrying firearms across the border (handguns are prohibited).

The alternative for defense is bear pepper spray. Leading bear authorities—including biologist Stephen Herrero; Chuck (Charles) Jonkel, director of the University of Montana's Border Grizzly Project; Barry Gilbert, an animal behavior and wildlife management specialist; and Gary Shelton—recommend that travelers in bear country carry pepper spray. Shelton, in his book *Bear Attacks: The Deadly Truth,* discourages tree climbing and submissive posturing as too dangerous, noting that several people each year are saved from serious injury or death by using bear pepper spray on charging bears.

But be forewarned. Nothing is 100 percent effective against the sudden, furious rush of an enraged bear—not a gun, not even bear pepper spray. The very best defense in bear country is to understand why bears attack and to avoid those situations that precipitate a confrontation.

CHAPTER 3

How I Learned
to Love Bear Pepper Spray

My first encounter with a problem bear occurred in the summer of 1970 while I was working for the Forest Service at the remote Red Ives Ranger Station in northern Idaho, where I was already known as a guy who was fascinated by bear behavior. One morning the cook, Esther Smith, asked me to shoot a black bear that had been tearing nightly at the door of her cookhouse.

The door's planks were badly chewed and clawed, and it was doubtful they could withstand another assault. Esther, who lived in a back room of the cookhouse, was at wit's end and wanted the bear killed, but I was reluctant to resort to such a drastic measure without first attempting some kind of aversive conditioning. My plan was to shoot the bear in the rump with a blunt arrow from my heavy hunting bow. There was no doubt in my mind that the arrow would send the bear on its way with lasting memories of the pain associated with the cookhouse.

At sundown, I got into my sleeping bag on the cookhouse floor and promptly fell asleep. I was jolted awake by loud grunting and the violent rattling of the door. I peeked out the side window to see a huge black bear, bathed in the harsh yellow porch light.

I yelled and pounded on the door, which sent the startled bear scrambling off the porch to the middle of the parking lot fifteen yards away. I slipped out to the porch and prepared to teach the bear a lesson. Taking careful aim, I released the arrow and the heavy shaft hit the bear's rump with a loud whump! Dust puffed up from the spot where the arrow hit. The bear jumped and spun around to inspect its rump but did not run away. I hastily nocked another blunt-tipped arrow onto the bow's string and this time aimed for the bear's shoulder. The arrow whacked the bear perfectly, but to my shock, the bear started walking toward me, head low and lolling, its gait stiff-legged. I barely made it back into the cookhouse before the bear, rushing forward, slammed against the door.

The next night I reluctantly shot the bear with a rifle. There were a lot of backslapping and thank-you's in the morning, which I graciously accepted, but inside I felt sad, for I could not reconcile the killing of such a magnificent animal for the crime of seeking food. As I watched a tractor drag the carcass off to a slit trench a half mile away, I told myself: *There has to be a better way to stop a bear than killing it.*

I began experimenting—with everything from ammonia in a squirt gun to a spud cannon—but nothing proved satisfactory. I dropped the project when my wildlife photography hobby turned into a profession and I began selling photos regularly to outdoor magazines. When I moved to grizzly country several years later, the issue of how to stop a bear resurfaced in a much more personal way when I was suddenly confronted not only with saving a bear's life, but also my own.

■ ■ ■

My first encounter with a grizzly occurred in Yellowstone National Park in June 1982 during a photography trip. The high-country meadows were full of cow elk nursing their calves. Those first few weeks were hazardous for the wobbly-legged calves because predators like coyotes, mountain lions, and bears cruised the birthing areas like land sharks, wreaking a terrible toll on the newborn.

I took off on foot from my pickup at dawn on a glorious early summer morning. My plan was to arrive at a meadow two miles away and photograph the elk as the first golden-amber rays of sunlight spread across the green grass. And if a grizzly appeared in the meadow, so much the better for my photos.

I followed open ridge tops to avoid stumbling upon a bear. The only tricky part was a two-hundred-yard stretch of creek bottom choked with brush and downed trees. To alert any bear of my presence, I yelled and sang as I entered the draw. When I was sixty yards from the open ridge I planned to follow, I stopped making noise. My eyes were already searching ahead for a game trail to follow out of the creek bottom.

A branch snapped in front of me, and I skidded to a halt. Standing broadside in the middle of the brushy trail fifty yards away was a sow grizzly and two cubs. My immediate thought was, *Oh no! I'm in big trouble!* Before I could react further, the two cubs scrambled away over blown-down timber and the smallish sow scampered after them.

At the meadow, I ran through four rolls of film before the

elk wandered off into the timber to bed down for the day. I sat on a rock outcrop and pondered the encounter with the sow and two cubs. *Maybe,* I thought, *these grizzlies are not as dangerous as everyone claims.*

An encounter two days later would correct that dangerous misconception. Early that morning I was hiking through an alpine area next to a timbered ridge below Dunraven Pass. I looked to the west and spotted a dark brown grizzly bear. The bear was so far away, about three hundred yards, that I doubted it could even see me, so I continued hiking at a brisk pace.

The wind shifted toward the bear, and a minute later I noticed that it was looking my way. Surely, I thought, that bear can't be looking at me from so far away. The bear stood on its hind legs, then dropped down and started galloping my way. My initial thought was that it was a coincidence. Then it struck me. The bear was coming for me!

I dashed to a tall lodgepole pine forty yards away and shinnied about fifteen feet up the tree. When I looked down, the bear was already there, glaring up at me. It circled the tree several times, growling and popping its teeth. Then it wandered off, as if nothing had happened.

For the next few months I roamed the wilds, now harboring difficult emotions, confused about the type of beast I was dealing with. Was a typical grizzly the frightened animal I'd vanquished just by my presence? Or was the true grizzly the powerful, determined beast that had treed me?

That fall I hiked five miles up the long trail to Huckleberry Mountain on the western edge of Glacier National Park to photograph grizzly bears feasting on frost-sweetened huckleberries. It was there that I met a slightly taciturn but very interesting fellow.

His name was Doug Peacock, and he would soon become widely known for his book *Grizzly Years*—a touching, troubling, terrifying manifesto about the camaraderie of being one with the great bear—even if that feeling wasn't always reciprocated. But at the time, Doug was just a lowly park employee manning the Huckleberry Mountain lookout tower.

I explained my confusion about grizzlies and began asking Doug questions about bear behavior. I learned more about grizzlies from Doug Peacock in two days than from all the bear books I've read since.

The mountain was swarming with grizzlies. At times we could see as many as a dozen bears. Doug pointed out a bear and said, "That's a young sow with cubs. She runs from everything."

But then, as if realizing that a little knowledge in the hands of a neophyte could be dangerous, he added, "Stay away from the sows. No telling what state they're in. The boars are always after the cubs. That's why the sows are half nuts all the time."

Then he pointed to a smallish bear feeding alone, and said, "That's a teenager. Just kicked out from his momma. He'll run, too."

Finally he pointed to a distant sidehill and directed my attention to a large, dark grizzly contentedly stripping berries and leaves from bushes. "Man, what a bear!" he exclaimed. "He's a big old boar. He figures the whole mountain is his. Yesterday a big bull moose came over the ridge, and that old bear chased the damn moose almost all the way down to the Camas Road. You walk into that bear, you're in trouble."

With his glasses still on the bear, Doug asked, "By the way, how'd you get up here so quick this morning?"

"I hiked about two hours in the dark," I proudly volunteered. "The trail was easy to follow."

"Yeah, well," Doug said, "you keep doin' that and you're gonna get in trouble." He lowered his binoculars and pointed a wagging finger toward the big old boar. Further explanation was unnecessary.

That sobering lesson on bear behavior, plus a few harrowing grizzly encounters, convinced me that I had to change my ways in bear country. I quit hiking in the dark, stayed away from trails that entered dense cover, and avoided areas of heavy bear activity. Still, whenever I roamed bear country, there was an uneasiness—a feeling that I was not in control and that my well-being depended largely on fate and chance. It took much of the enjoyment out of my recreation and photography trips, but at the time, nothing short of a gun could provide any sense of security.

■ ■ ■

During this period, I'd taken a job with Stoney-Wolf Video Productions as a scriptwriter and videographer. The company was expanding its line of outdoor videos to include a nature series, and I was asked to write a script for a video about staying safe in bear country. While working on this project, I had met Mark Matheny, owner of UDAP, a manufacturer of bear-deterrent pepper spray.

I test-fired a can of Mark's pepper in a woodlot behind our office and was surprised by the volume, range, and noise of the spray. As the orange mist slowly drifted back toward me, I became fascinated by it—and curious to see how it might affect me. The next thing I knew, I was on the ground, howling! My eyes felt like they were on fire. My nose and mouth burned fiercely. It took half an hour before I was able to function again.

The other members of the video crew and I joked about my

mishap, but deep inside I was wildly excited: I'd discovered a way to protect myself if a wild animal attacked.

I've since used my bear spray three times: twice on aggressive black bears and once on a mountain lion. The first bear incident occurred in western Montana while I was photographing a 150-pound black bear. I had maintained a respectable distance from the bear, but then it began ambling toward me. I yelled and slowly retreated. The bear stopped about forty feet away, sat on its haunches, and turned baleful eyes on me.

My bear spray was out and ready. The bear lunged forward and swatted the ground. I sent a huge blast of spray at the bear, but the animal was a bit out of range. However, the loud hissing noise and the huge ball of orange mist startled the bear and it grabbed a tree, as if ready to climb it. I sprayed it again, and this time the spray got to the bear. The bruin shook its head and stumbled away, wheezing.

The next bear incident occurred two years later in late spring while I was hiking up a mountain trail. I came around a corner and startled two large, adult black bears preparing to mate. Both bears ambled up the trail, and one bear finally bounded down through the brush as the other stood eyeing me forty yards away. I yelled and waved my arms, but the bear kept walking toward me. With my pepper spray out, I yelled again. The bear stopped and sat down, giving me that familiar baleful stare. Then it began slowly walking toward me again, stiff-legged and swaggering. I yelled, and the bear stopped again about forty feet away. The air currents were pushing uphill toward the bear, so I decided to give it a dose of aversive conditioning. The orange cloud of bear pepper spray enveloped the bear's head. The bruin made a gagging noise, pawed at its face, and staggered below the trail, stopping often to rub its face on the ground.

■ ■ ■

I've seen the awesome results of bear spray. Now I not only feel safe when confronted by an aggressive large predator, but I also feel confident striding through the deepest wilderness. Many a night I have curled up under a tree in the backcountry, secure in the knowledge that there was little to fear. All because of a can of bear spray close at hand.

The deterrent potential of that can on my belt has allowed me to think rationally during periods of intense stress. Knowing that this potent weapon was at my side, ready for use, kept me focused during a night I spent in serious danger from a couple of angry, hungry bears.

The incident occurred during a 1998 elk archery hunt when I'd hiked alone into a remote wilderness area in northwest Colorado's Routt National Forest. On the afternoon of my first day, I set up camp and rested there until shadows grew long. Then I dropped down a long ridge to a series of small side ridges. On the second ridge, I bugled—simulating the mating call of a bull elk—and a bull bugled back from 150 yards away. Within minutes, the bull was just twenty-five yards from me, angrily raking his antlers on a red fir sapling.

I bugled again, and the bull bellowed a furious challenge. Suddenly his enormous rack of antlers appeared above the trees and started moving toward me. When the bull stepped into a small opening eighteen yards below me, I cow-called, mimicking the soft, birdlike chirp of a cow elk, and the huge animal stopped. His eyes were just beginning to register alarm when my razor-sharp arrow zipped through his chest. The startled animal staggered, then galloped off into the dense forest below. Ten minutes later I found the magnificent animal lying dead in a bed of ferns and aspen trees.

In keeping with the Native American custom of thanksgiving, I thanked the elk for giving himself to me, and I assured him that his meat and hide would be used to feed my family and provide clothing and shoes. Then I kissed the coarse, dark-brown hair on the elk's neck and bid him good-bye.

I quickly field-dressed the elk and hung the quarters in aspen trees to cool off, but by the time I'd finished, it was past sundown. It would have been foolish to attempt hiking back to camp in the dark, so I crawled under a large spruce tree forty yards from the elk carcass and prepared to spend the night.

Wearing a poncho and sheltered beneath a space blanket, I curled up under the tree as dark settled upon the forest. About midnight, the first patter of rain hit the space blanket, and soon a cold wind blew torrents of heavy rain against my little shelter, but I stayed snug and warm underneath. I thought I heard sounds around me, but I shrugged them off and fell asleep.

Suddenly I was awake. I'd heard a sound that raised the hair on the back of my neck. My ears strained to pick up any new fragment of sound that would help me identify it. The sound came again, and this time I recognized it, loud and clear, ominous and frightening. It was the sound of powerful jaws crushing bone.

I threw back the space blanket and flipped on my flashlight. The beam picked up the elk quarters hanging in the trees, then shone on the glowing eyes of a huge black bear. I yelled and threw tree limbs at the bear, and it ran off. I retreated under the space blanket, hoping that was the end of it. It was just the beginning.

Ten minutes later the bear returned, grunting and biting at the carcass. This time it refused to leave when I yelled at it, and

I was forced to huddle at my shelter while the bear fed on my elk. Suddenly a furious bawling erupted, followed by snapping teeth and the heavy thud of large bodies pounding through the brush. I thought the bear was coming for me, so I threw back the space blanket, bear pepper spray up and ready.

The tremendous commotion continued down by the carcass. My flashlight picked up two bears roaring at each other, the larger one occasionally chasing the smaller one around the carcass. For the rest of the night I endured the nearby rampage, unable to sleep, bear spray in hand, just in case. Several times I considered running back up the ridge, but such a move would have been foolhardy in that cold, driving rain. Though I was damp, the poncho and space blanket kept me relatively comfortable. The bears eventually left.

At dawn I started a small fire and dried out, then moved down to the elk carcass to assess the damage. The forest was trampled for twenty yards around the carcass, which had been pulled downhill about thirty yards by the bears. I hastily packed the remains of the elk quarters a hundred yards farther up the ridge. When I arrived to pack out the last quarter, a large black bear sow with two cubs was at the carcass and watched me with alarm, torn between fleeing and gorging on the leftovers. Finally, they drifted off into the forest and I hurried away with the last of the meat.

In my opinion, that can of bear spray saved my life. It gave me the security of knowing that I could stop the bears if they tried to attack me. It permitted me the confidence and clear thinking to stay put instead of trying to flee up the ridge through heavy brush in a cold rain, with a good possibility of getting lost, and hypothermia almost guaranteed.

■ ■ ■

Being an extrovert and certified blabbermouth, I began spreading the great news about pepper spray with religious zeal. I became a regular speaker at seminars on self-defense for nature lovers. As I extolled the effectiveness of bear pepper spray as a deterrent, I was continually taken aback by the ignorance of my audience on the subject and by the misinformation they had absorbed. In a nutshell, folks doubted the stopping power of bear pepper spray, and no matter how much I spoke up for it, there were those in the audience who remained skeptical.

I needed something that would graphically illustrate the stopping power of bear spray. I couldn't use firsthand testimony: the two bears and the mountain lion that I sprayed didn't stick around for an interview. And my accidental spraying of myself had not been recorded—and was only a slight exposure compared with receiving a full dose in the face. I needed someone gullible (and dumb!) enough to run into a blast of bear spray and to then describe, on video, what it feels like. I searched the entire world and found only one person dumb enough to attempt such a stunt. Me!

On a clear spring day in Montana, I stood fifty yards away from a friend who held a large can of bear-deterrent pepper spray in his hand. I dropped into a low crouch and came fast, like a bear. My friend held off until I was about forty feet away. I saw a beautiful orange cloud come out to greet me. Next thing I knew, I was on the ground, gasping for air. My eyes felt like a thousand needles were poking them. My nose and mouth burned like fire, and I could breathe only in short, ragged gasps.

The object of this folly was to talk to the camera immediately afterward and to explain what it felt like to be sprayed. But I was unable to speak, and for the next thirty minutes I could do nothing but try to survive, because the red pepper caused excruciating burning to my face. As I suffered, the camera kept rolling. After thirty minutes, and with the liberal application of aloe vera gel, the effects had largely worn off, and within fifty minutes I felt almost normal.

When I show this video at my seminars, the audience becomes still. Few skeptics remain after seeing the painful, debilitating effects a single airborne cloud of red-hot pepper had on me, making it easy to visualize the effects it would have on a charging bear.

Important note: Allowing myself to be doused with bear-deterrent pepper spray grew out of my sincere desire to convince skeptical people of its effectiveness. I hope this stunt will never be duplicated by another human. It was an excruciatingly painful experience that I will never try again. Bear-deterrent pepper spray is made to stop bears; it should never be used on humans, even in self-defense. (Personal-defense pepper spray is sold in diluted form in a smaller can.)

Chapter 4

The Remarkable Story
of Bear-Deterrent Spray

C all it providence, but the first night Bill Pounds spent in Montana was a terrifying experience. A grizzly bear invaded his camp, pawing at his gear and sniffing at his tent. Bill recalls, "When I realized it was a bear, I was very alarmed. My hair stood on end. I had a small pistol with me, but I felt such a sense of inadequacy and vulnerability. It was as bad as anything I'd experienced when I was in Vietnam."

Bill fell in love with Montana and planned to move his family there, but he was determined his wife and children would never be exposed to the terror he'd experienced that first night. An entrepreneur and innovator by nature, Bill began a search for some chemical or device that would stop a bear. In the meantime, he customized a shotgun for his wife, but with small children in the house, she didn't want to have it around.

In trying to find the ideal bear deterrent, Bill experimented with less lethal solutions, such as ammonia and water, without success. After three years, he was sitting alone in his office one night, feeling the weight of defeat. He was burned out. He needed a vacation.

He sat up abruptly, thinking back to his last vacation down in old Mexico and remembering a painful joke the locals had played on him. His pulse quickened as he rummaged through his memory. The incident had occurred at a cantina in an isolated fishing village along the Gulf Coast. Bill's easygoing personality had made him readily accepted as a regular at the local bar. One night the leader of the locals offered him a small red pepper and a large glass of beer, announcing loudly, "Señor, we bring you a gift of honor."

Bill studied the men with narrowed eyes. They were tough hombres who routinely caroused at the backstreet cantinas. It was against their nature to suddenly become so simpatico.

"Drink up, my friend," the leader announced with a mischievous grin. "Try this delicious fruit from my wife's garden. It will solve your immediate problems."

Bill surrounded the glass of beer with his meaty hand, then gingerly picked up the innocuous-looking pepper, studying its deep crimson sheen. He was reminded of a favorite saying of his smaller comrades: "Dangerous things come in small packages." The men crowded around him, some of them exchanging knowing glances.

He put the pepper to his nose and sniffed. Its sweet, pungent fragrance reminded him of the many times he'd whiffed the same aroma at his favorite pasta house. He put the pepper in his mouth and touched it with his tongue. Nothing. Then he nipped the very end with his teeth.

"Aiiy!" he bellowed as his lips and gums turned to fire. He

washed his mouth with the beer, then had another, but the fire in his mouth still seared his flesh.

He jumped up and grasped the ringleader's arm. "What is this stuff?" he bellowed between gulps of beer.

The man shrugged his shoulders and replied with a mischievous grin, "Just cayenne, Señor."

■ ■ ■

Chuck (Charles) Jonkel, director of the University of Montana's Border Grizzly Project, was also struggling in a search for a bear repellent. In his attempt to find something short of a shotgun blast that would stop an aggressive grizzly, he had experimented with gimmicks—loud music, a black umbrella, foghorns, balloons—and with chemicals, including mothballs, ammonia, and human urine. Nothing had worked.

The previous month, a man had rushed into his office and announced that he'd discovered the perfect bear deterrent. He stuck a bottle under Chuck's nose and twisted off the cap. It took two hours with all the windows open to clear the putrid odor of skunk urine from the building.

Despite the horrible odor, Chuck agreed to test it on grizzly bears held in captivity. It didn't work. Unlike humans, animals are attracted to the odor of skunk. For centuries, fur trappers have used skunk scent mixed into their lures to attract furbearers to their traps. When Chuck told the man that the skunk urine tests had failed, the man stomped angrily out of the office.

It was only natural that Chuck Jonkel looked upon Bill Pounds with thinly veiled skepticism when Bill pulled out a tiny red pepper and announced that he had discovered the perfect bear deterrent.

Chuck sighed heavily and studied the little pepper. At least he wouldn't have to evacuate the building if it didn't work.

But Bill had more to show Chuck. He had paid a Florida company one hundred dollars to load concentrated pepper spray into five aerosol spray cans.

One small exposure to the contents of a spray can was all it took to convince Chuck—after he could see and breathe again. "We tested the pepper spray on sixty black and grizzly bears in captivity," Chuck said. "It never failed to make a bear stop what it was doing." During this process, Bill changed the formula several times, making the pepper base stronger and developing better aerosol systems.

"Our greatest challenge was in canceling a bear's rage factor," Bill said. "This rage factor in a grizzly is high, along with its tolerance to pain. We worked hard to increase the pepper concentration to get it so hot it would cancel the bear's rage factor and force it into a survival mode. That could only occur if it couldn't see or breathe, and the pain was so severe that it wanted to get away from the source. Red pepper spray passed these tests with flying colors.

"We accomplished with pepper spray what a shotgun blast did, blinding the charging bear. But the effects of the pepper spray went away in less than an hour, and there was no wounded bear to have to deal with."

Bill Pounds mentioned that, although he was the first to experiment with pepper spray in defense against bears, the Chinese already had been using pepper spray in a fine powder form on people to quell disturbances. At the time Bill was experimenting, pepper spray was not yet in the arsenal of U.S. police, who were still relying on Mace and tear gas.

It took six years of testing and perfecting pepper spray before Bill felt confident that he had a marketable product. After six hundred tests without a failure, he founded the company Counter Assault in 1986. Chuck Jonkel said, "Someone may come up with a miracle cure tomorrow, but for now, pepper spray is the best thing out there to stop an aggressive bear."

Of course, lab and zoo animal tests were one thing. It still remained to be proven how well pepper spray would work on a wild aggressive bear. Bill sent a sample can to John Hyde, a bear specialist with the Alaska Department of Fish and Game. John was understandably skeptical, but he got in the habit of throwing the can into his pack whenever he went afield.

One day while working along the shore of Admiralty Island, John noticed a large grizzly sow aggressively approaching a pair of kayakers. Though he was unarmed, John hurried to aid them. The men yelled and threw things at the bear, but she continued toward them. When the sow was only ten feet away, bluff-charging and snapping her teeth, John sprayed the bear full in the face. She somersaulted backward and ran a hundred yards before stopping to look back.

Two days later John encountered the bear again, and when the sow was still fifty feet away, he sprayed toward the bear. The orange cloud did not reach the sow, but when she walked into it, she immediately bawled and ran off. The next day when he saw the same sow fifty yards away, he merely raised the can and the bear galloped off.

■ ■ ■

During the early years that bear pepper spray was on the market, several companies began producing weak sprays that often fizzled out of the can and failed to stop a charging bear. Bad publicity from the failures of these inferior sprays lingers today in the public's skepticism of the effectiveness of bear spray.

In 1996 the Environmental Protection Agency (EPA) became involved because red pepper is an organic compound. To be registered as a bear-deterrent pepper spray, the EPA requires a pepper spray manufacturer to follow stringent guidelines for ingredients, performance, and accuracy in advertising. While there are about twenty manufacturers of personal-defense and police-use pepper sprays, only six bear-deterrent sprays are registered with the EPA. They are Counter Assault, UDAP Pepper Power, Bear Guard, Bear Peppermace, Frontiersman, and Guard Alaska. Personal-defense pepper spray is much more diluted than bear spray and should never be considered as a substitute for EPA-registered bear spray.

Contrary to popular belief, pepper spray is not ground-up cayenne peppers in spray form. This would never make it out of the can's tiny nozzle. EPA-registered pepper sprays contain about 10 percent (by weight) oleoresin of capsicum (OC), which is the oil derived from the pepper. However, the EPA does not allow registered sprays to list the OC on the can because it is a misleading gauge of a pepper spray's hotness. Instead, it is the capsaicin and related capsaicinoids (CRC) found in OC that make it hot and are the true measure of a pepper spray's strength. The EPA requires between 1 and 2 percent CRC in its approved bear-deterrent sprays. Most of the EPA-registered sprays are right at, or very close to, 2 percent.

When inert, red pepper is innocuous. But when it comes into

contact with body tissue where moisture is present, its ingredients act as an extreme irritant. Used in tiny amounts as a spice, the effect is to add zing to foods. Red pepper may cause no discomfort against dry skin, but it causes an instant fiery sensation in eyes, mouth, and nose. When breathed into the lungs, pepper spray instantly swells mucus membranes, shutting down all but life-support breathing.

EPA-approved sprays shoot out of the can in a shotgunlike fog about thirty feet long and ten feet wide that tends to hang in the air. The object is to lay out this orange screen of capsaicin-laced oil between yourself and the charging bear so the animal will run into it, feel its effects, and abort the attack.

Bear-deterrent pepper spray does not come out of the can in a soft mist like some aerosols. It is under tremendous pressure—about one hundred pounds in a twelve-ounce can—that pushes the capsaicin out thirty feet in a microsecond. The cans are one-piece aluminum containers that use O-ring gaskets and high-impact plastic parts.

When the trigger is depressed, the spray shoots out of the can with a startlingly loud *spooow!* Almost as loud as a .22 rifle, the noise alone has scared away large predators.

■ ■ ■

In 1998, Tom Smith, a wildlife ecologist for the U.S. Geological Survey, noticed that some people in his area of Alaska were applying bear spray to boats and oars and other items they wanted to keep safe from marauding bears. Tom also noticed that the bears, rather than being repelled, actually sought out the bright orange pepper, often sniffing it and rolling in it.

He mentioned this phenomenon in a short news release, hoping to correct a simple misconception about bear spray. He wanted the public to know that the spray, while highly effective when shot at an animal, has no value as a repellent sprayed on other objects.

Newspapers took the news release and blew it into a misleading—and greatly damaging—issue. Headlines read: "Researcher Discovers Pepper Spray Actually Attracts Bears." The full articles were more factual, but readers mostly remembered the sensational headlines.

The confusion might have died down except for the misguided efforts of a relative newcomer to the lucrative bear pepper spray market. Chem-Armor, which manufactures Bear Paws pepper spray, began discrediting other pepper sprays. The company claimed it used only the capsicum, and none of the vegetable oils, vitamins, and minerals used in other products.

In an e-mail to the EPA, Chem-Armor chemist Cody Dwyer contended that competing pepper sprays actually attract bears because they use food-grade oleoresin of capsicum. "These food-based sprays are more stinky than bacon grease," Dwyer said. He mentioned a Japanese-American photographer who had been attacked and killed in Russia while he slept outside a cabin where red pepper spray had been sprayed on the ground.

This further added to the alarm and confusion, until the EPA stepped in and banned Bear Paws from store shelves because it was using an unproven synthetic form of oleoresin of capsicum and marketing it as bear spray. The Interagency Grizzly Bear Committee, which includes many of the top bear experts in North America, came out with a strong statement that said, "Pepper spray is amazingly useful in repelling bear attacks—and does not, as

Chem-Armor contends, attract bears to campsites." Experts, however, do advise against releasing bear spray around a campsite except in direct use on an aggressive bear, because in its inert form—as Tom Smith discovered—it can actually appeal to a bear.

U.S. Forest Service bear habitat coordinator Jay Gore said, "You don't use bear spray like it's an insect repellent. It's stupid to spray your kids, your tent. It's supposed to be used as an airborne deterrent in a bear attack."

Chuck Bartlebaugh, director of the Center for Wildlife Information, in Missoula, Montana, added, "Any synthetic attracts bears: tents, yellow rain slickers, a camera lens cap." Bartlebaugh accused Chem-Armor of "fear marketing." He also noted that the photographer who died in Russia was sleeping outside a cabin in an area where habituated brown bears roamed, having been fed by other photographers seeking better pictures.

The efforts of the EPA and leading bear experts helped quiet the furor over the false idea that properly used bear pepper spray attracts bears. But among people who only remember the headlines, the misconception continues today.

And what of Tom Smith, the man whose news release started the whole thing? Tom stated he wouldn't be caught dead in the backcountry without bear spray. Or maybe he would be, because as Tom said of bear pepper spray, "It saved my bacon more than a couple of times."

■ ■ ■

A bear attack usually occurs quickly. A hiker walks around a corner on a trail, a startled bear spots the hiker, and the bear charges. You may have only seconds to react. For that reason, it's not prudent to carry bear pepper spray in a backpack or anywhere else where it can't be ready for use within three seconds. Essentially, that means using a hip, shoulder, or chest holster that allows quick, easy access.

California resident Kelly Krpata learned that lesson the hard way on a warm August morning in the year 2000 while he and a companion, Kim Taffer, were hiking east along Swiftcurrent Pass Trail in Glacier National Park. Kelly was in the lead when he startled a grizzly fifty yards away. The bear immediately charged. Kelly didn't have time to get his bear spray out, so he dropped into a fetal position just before the bear hit him. Kim curled up in some bushes not far off the trail and was not noticed by the bear.

The attack lasted just ten seconds before the bear lumbered off into the brush near Bullhead Lake. Kelly suffered leg and hip injuries and his backpack and sleeping bag were shredded. A half hour after the attack, a park ranger walking the trail heard calls for help and administered first aid. A horse was brought in to carry Kelly to the trailhead, where a waiting ambulance rushed him to a hospital.

Bears can run amazingly fast, with a top speed of about thirty-five miles per hour. Even though bear pepper spray has a range of thirty feet, don't wait until the bear is at that range to spray it. Instead, shoot a one-second burst when the charging bear is about fifty to sixty feet away. The heavy, orange cloud will hang in the air and act as a screen that the bear must pass through. This usually stops the animal, forcing it to abandon its attack and flee the source of the sudden pain.

If that first cloud of spray misses the charging bear or does not deter it, shoot a heavy dose for about two seconds right into the bear's face. Many attack survivors have sprayed bears in full charge at less than ten feet. These bears skidded to an instant stop, gagging and coughing and pawing at their faces, and then ran away—sometimes stumbling into trees as they fled.

■ ■ ■

Users of bear pepper spray need to guard against accidents. A child playing with a can of the spray is going to learn a very painful lesson if it discharges, but no fatal injury will likely result (although for half an hour the youngster may think death is on the way). People with asthma should be especially careful to avoid coming into contact with bear spray because of its severe effects on breathing.

Some bear-spray accidents are partly attributable to the fact that the can resembles a variety of common household spray containers. Also, the knowledge that the red pepper does not usually inflict fatal injury may lull the user into a lackadaisical attitude.

While on a bowhunting trip in Alaska, outdoorsman Monte Morovac learned the hard way to be careful with pepper spray. As he walked along a glacier-fed river, he bent down and accidentally depressed the trigger on the can of bear spray he had jammed into a pants pocket.

Before he could extricate the can, it had soaked his groin area. His private parts instantly felt like they were on fire, and Monte jumped into the ice-cold river up to his waist. After five minutes, hypothermia became the more immediate danger, so he hopped out to warm up, but then his groin burned again, so he jumped back into the water again. He hopped in and out of the water for almost an hour before the effects of the bear pepper spray wore off.

The best treatment for an accidental spraying is to wash off the oily residue as quickly as possible. Warm soapy water will cut the oil and remove the pepper. Though you'll still have to endure some pain, the severity and duration will be lessened considerably. The gel of aloe vera is an excellent treatment for afflicted skin.

Wind drift is a major concern when you shoot bear pepper spray, because a wind moving in your direction may carry the airborne spray back to you. You can help counteract wind drift simply by stepping backward immediately after you spray. In fact, no matter which direction the wind is blowing, you should retreat several paces to get farther away from the attacking bear. As you travel, keep aware of the wind's direction. The simplest way to confirm wind direction is to wet the tip of your index finger and raise it above your head; even a slight breeze will cause that side of your finger to feel cool.

Doug MacCartney, a Yellowstone National Park employee from Gardner, Montana, was charged by a grizzly bear while walking into a stiff wind, and his experience with bear pepper spray is worth noting. On September 9, 2000, Doug hiked into remote Pelican Valley with his wife, Joanne, and her friend Jane Cunningham. Their destination for the night was a cabin eleven miles up the valley.

The trail meandered through open sagebrush for the first five miles, then entered forest. As the hikers approached a water hole a quarter mile into the timber, a flock of ravens and two golden eagles flew up. The women were thrilled to see the huge eagles so close, but the presence of the scavenging birds concerned Doug.

"We better be careful," he remarked. "Might be a carcass nearby."

They stopped to fill their canteens. Joanne left the group for a few seconds to answer a call of nature and stumbled upon a bull elk carcass. She hurried back and told Doug. He examined the carcass, which had been picked over but still gave off quite an odor. "We better get away from here," Doug warned, "before a bear finds it."

After a night at the cabin, the three hikers started back. A half mile from the carcass, they noticed a large boar grizzly moving toward that area.

They circled the water hole, staying about two hundred yards away and making lots of noise as they hiked. With Joanne and Jane a few steps in the lead, Doug was startled by a loud crash ahead. He looked up and saw a large sow grizzly and three cubs hurrying onto an open ridge a hundred and fifty yards away. Doug alerted the women and called them back to him.

"I've encountered lots of grizzlies in Yellowstone," Doug said later. "At that time, I felt we were in no danger, what with the sow being so far away. She had lots of room to move off without feeling threatened."

But as the women hurried to the rear, Doug watched the sow run to within a hundred yards of them. The animal stopped and stood up, sniffing the air. When she caught their scent, she dropped down and charged.

Joanne and Jane were about ten feet behind Doug. He pulled out his bear pepper spray and warned them to get their spray ready. He had been paying attention to the wind throughout the hike, so he knew that the wind had shifted and now a stiff breeze faced them. He gave himself a quick reminder: *There'll be some wind drift, so be sure to step back if you have to spray.*

The sow disappeared from sight into a deep gully, and Doug thought she would probably turn and follow it away from them. All was quiet for a few seconds, and he began to feel a sense of relief. Suddenly the sow burst over the ridge forty yards away, galloping toward him. When the grizzly was about forty feet away Doug shot a short burst of bear spray, hoping the screen of spray would stop her.

The first shot was only partially successful because the stiff wind sent it drifting to the left. Still, it halted the sow's charge. She raised up, then dropped down and lunged at Doug. The sow was only ten feet away and coming fast, mouth agape and beady eyes full of rage, when he blasted her full in the face for two seconds. The sow jerked backward, gagging. At that moment, Doug became aware that Joanne and Jane were also spraying the bear from behind him.

That's the last thing Doug saw because the bear pepper spray engulfed him and burned his eyes. He frantically blinked his eyes open and finally located the sow grizzly standing about fifty feet away, experiencing much the same pain as Doug. Finally the sow turned and stumbled back into the gully, with her cubs close behind.

By now the bear spray had drifted back to the women, and they also experienced some burning to their faces and eyes. But the group was able to function well enough to quickly hike in the opposite direction from that taken by the sow. They hiked in silence for half a mile until they came to a stream, where they washed the spray from their hands and faces.

Soon, Joanne and Jane were almost over their discomfort, and Doug began feeling better. The women even laughed about all the orange spray they had shot on the butt and legs of Doug's jeans.

As they hurried away under the warm sun, Doug started feeling a burning sensation on his back, his buttocks, and the backs of his legs. It was then he realized his mistake. His sweaty skin had made contact with the bear pepper spray on his outer clothing. To make matters worse, bear spray on his hair now mixed with sweat and ran down his face and into his eyes.

He was in agony and virtually blind before they reached the next stream. He tore off his clothes and jumped into the frigid waters. After half an hour of cleaning his skin and rinsing his clothes, he was able to get dressed and begin hiking again.

Doug was still feeling the effects of the bear spray when he phoned his mother a few hours later: "Mom, it feels like I have the world's worst sunburn."

"Well," his mother said, "what do you do when you have a bad sunburn?"

Doug thought for a second, then answered, "I put aloe vera on it."

The pain left soon after Doug rubbed the aloe vera onto his skin.

Doug MacCartney summed up his bear encounter: "Actually, for as stiff as that wind was blowing, the wind drift wasn't as bad as I would have expected. The women experienced some smarting in their eyes and faces, but they were never blinded, and it went away pretty quickly. My problem was that they covered me when they sprayed past me at the bear. Sure, it hurt for a while, but I shudder to think of the pain and damage that sow would have inflicted on me, and maybe all of us, if we didn't have the pepper spray."

Doug was more bothered by the uncharacteristic reaction of the sow. "I would have bet money she wouldn't charge from that far away. My guess is that the big boar we saw earlier must have made a try for her cubs, and when we encountered her, she was in such an enraged state that she would have charged anything that moved."

■ ■ ■

In spite of the many instances of people being saved by bear pepper spray, most hikers in the two U.S. national parks with the most grizzlies—Glacier and Yellowstone—continue to hike without this protection. In an effort to understand why more people traveling in bear country don't carry bear pepper spray, I traveled backcountry trails in Yellowstone and Glacier and talked with many hikers.

I interviewed 346 hikers—227 in Glacier and 119 in Yellowstone. Only 34 people—25 in Glacier and 9 in Yellowstone—were carrying bear pepper spray. Nine out of ten people were hiking defenseless through some of the densest concentrations of grizzlies in North America.

The reasons given were even more disturbing. A majority of the hikers said they didn't know there were grizzly bears in the area. That blew me away. Every turnoff, trailhead, campground, and picnic area in Glacier and Yellowstone are plastered with orange signs showing a humped bear advancing menacingly, warning the reader of the presence of grizzly bears.

In Glacier, I interviewed a man from Wisconsin on the loop trail to Granite Park Chalet. He smirked and quipped that he'd been looking for grizzlies but couldn't find any. He figured they were found on the more remote trails. I informed him that just a mile away on this same trail, a man had been killed by a bear—a man from Wisconsin.

My most amazing interview was with two counselors who

were leading six boys on a twelve-mile hike from Logan Pass, past Granite Park Chalet, and down to the Loop, Glacier's most popular hiking trail. Both counselors were totally ignorant of the presence of bears in the area. They had almost no knowledge of bear spray or bear-attack survival techniques, such as playing dead or rolling into a fetal position.

Though ignorance of the presence and potential danger of bears ran high, misconceptions over the effectiveness of bear pepper spray were the leading cause of folks hiking defenseless through bear country. The number-one reason for not carrying bear spray was the misconception, voiced by almost half of those interviewed, that it actually attracted bears, even when carried unfired in a holster. It is amazing how one misleading newspaper story had reached into the heart of America and inadvertently done so much damage.

Some people objected to the price. After spending hundreds, often thousands, of dollars to travel to a national park, people resisted spending forty dollars for a product that not only made them safer but also afforded peace of mind for themselves and their loved ones.

I endured some cute quips along the way. "Aw, pepper spray just gives you a six-second head start on a bear," I was told. Another favorite was, "I don't have to outrun a bear. I just have to outrun the guy next to me. Ha! Ha!"

But I also met people who became frightened, visibly trembling, when they finally realized they were in the wilderness, deep in bear country, with no means of defending themselves. I ended up handing out seven cans of bear pepper spray to frightened folks with children.

■ ■ ■

Stephen Herrero, author of the book *Bear Attacks*, was once tepid in his recommendation of bear pepper spray. Since then, he has become a strong advocate. To help determine the effectiveness of bear spray, Herrero surveyed 235 agencies that have jurisdiction over black or grizzly bears or whose employees frequent bear habitat.

His question to these agencies was basic and precise: *What are the known reactions of free-ranging, and aggressive, or curious, or human-conditioned black or grizzly bears who have been sprayed with aerosols containing 10 percent capsicum?*

These agencies—including the U.S.D.A. Forest Service, the National Park Service, and other state, federal, and provincial wildlife agencies—responded with sixty-six cases of field use of these sprays between 1984 and 1994.

The agencies reported sixteen cases in which the sprays were used during sudden encounters with aggressive grizzly bears (including the grizzlies known as brown bears). In every instance but one, the spray had the effect of stopping the bear from doing whatever it was doing at the moment it was sprayed. However, six of the bears continued to act aggressively, and in three of these cases the bear attacked the person spraying. Of the three encounters that resulted in injury, two involved a sow with cubs and the other involved a single bear. In all three injury incidents, the bear received a substantial dose of spray in the face. While it can't be known for certain how these sixteen encounters would have ended in the absence of bear pepper spray, the use of spray appears to have prevented injury in most cases.

Twenty incidents involved grizzly (or brown) bears that simply appeared to be curious or to be searching for human food or garbage. In all cases, the spray stopped the behavior the bear was displaying before it was sprayed. Eighteen of the bears left the area after a dousing with the spray, and only two of these eighteen later returned. No injuries to people were reported.

Four cases involved a sudden encounter with an aggressive black bear that may have been stalking a human as prey. The spray made each bear stop the behavior it was displaying immediately prior to being sprayed, although none of the bears left the area. No person was injured.

The agencies reported twenty-six black-bear incidents associated with curiosity or a search for human food or garbage. In nineteen cases, the spray stopped the bear's activity at the time it was doused. Only fourteen bears left the area after being sprayed, and six of these came back. No injuries to people were reported.

From this data, Herrero came to the following conclusions. However, he notes that because the information came from diverse field records, the results should be viewed with caution.

■ Capsaicin-based pepper spray appears to be reasonably, but not 100 percent, effective against aggressive grizzly/brown bears in sudden encounters.

■ Use of bear pepper spray against grizzly/brown bears searching for human food or garbage seems to be generally effective in causing the bears to stop and leave the area.

■ It isn't possible to draw conclusions about the effectiveness of the spray in sudden encounters with possibly predacious black bears. However, analysis of the small number of incidents—only four—suggests the spray is less effective than in sudden encounters with grizzly bears.

■ Use of the spray against black bears searching for human food or garbage is mixed in its effectiveness. The spray appears ineffective as a means of deterring black bears from returning to an area after they are strongly conditioned to human food or garbage.

■ In at least some bears, the spray doesn't cause such a severe physical reaction that the animal completely stops what it was doing before the spraying.

■ Pepper sprays containing capsaicin appear to be potentially useful in a variety of field situations.

Commercial bear-deterrent pepper spray has improved greatly over the years. The bear spray on store shelves today, thanks to the EPA, is better made and, most importantly, more reliable. It contains more accurate labeling, better propellants, and hotter pepper formulas. And as we can see from Herrero's survey, bear pepper spray users have experienced remarkable success in stopping aggressive bears.

However, Herrero also concluded that certain bears seem to have a high tolerance for bear pepper spray. There were a few instances in which bear spray failed to stop an aggressive predator. These spray failures should serve as a sobering reminder that the best way to avoid being attacked by a bear is to avoid potentially dangerous situations.

■ ■ ■

There are a number of do's and don'ts when it comes to bear spray. If you keep these in mind, the spray can be a valuable and possibly lifesaving component of your outdoor gear.

BEAR SPRAY DO'S

■ Do read the label before purchasing a can of spray; make sure it's labeled as a bear deterrent and carries an EPA registration number.

■ Do make sure the can contains a minimum of 7.9 ounces (or 225 grams).

■ Do make sure the contents include between 1 and 2 percent CRC (capsaicin and related capsaicinoids).

■ Do check the expiration date on the can.

■ Do test-fire your spray before going afield; wipe any excess residue from the nozzle.

■ Do practice removing the can from its holster and flipping off the safety tab.

■ Do transport spray in the trunk or rear compartment of a vehicle.

■ Do carry your spray in a quickly accessible holster when hiking

■ Do keep track of wind direction while hiking.

■ Do spray a charging bear when it is still fifty to sixty feet away, aiming a bit low so the spray will billow up to the bear's face.

■ Do continue spraying at the bear's face if the bear continues forward.

■ Do take a few steps backward to avoid spray drift after spraying.

BEAR SPRAY DON'TS

■ Don't purchase a non-EPA-registered spray.

■ Don't purchase a bear spray that is not labeled as a bear deterrent.

- Don't carry a small personal-defense pepper spray device to deter bears.
- Don't store spray anywhere in a vehicle. In summer, temperatures may cause the pressurized gas in the can to expand and rupture the can, and in winter, the freezing and thawing of bear spray in a can may eventually cause the ingredients to break down.
- Don't leave spray on a vehicle's dash, or in direct sunlight, or where the temperature may exceed 120°F.
- Don't carry spray in a backpack or anywhere else where it is not quickly accessible.
- Don't rely on someone else in your group to keep you safe; carry your own bear spray.
- Don't spray at a bear if it is beyond a range of thirty feet and is not aggressive or advancing.
- Don't spray personal items; the residue may attract bears.
- Don't spray other people. Bear spray is not a repellent. It will cause extreme pain to anyone who is sprayed, and the residue may attract bears.

CHAPTER 5

When Bear Pepper Spray Fails

B ear spray's success rate in stopping aggressive grizzly bears is impressive (about 90 percent, to judge by the survey conducted by Stephen Herrero and discussed in the previous chapter). But what about the 10 percent of cases in which bear spray doesn't stop the bear?

For people involved in these failures, it can mean an eye that's lopsided or missing. Or an angry red scar in a long, jagged line across a pretty face. It's a series of puncture wounds in the oval shape of a bear's jaws, or a slight limp to compensate for muscle torn away. It's the inability to ever again wear a swimsuit without embarrassment because of scars and missing flesh.

Fortunately, there are many more bear pepper spray success stories than failures. But a few of the incidents in which bear spray apparently failed to stop a charging bear are worth examining so we can glean some understanding of what happened and why.

■ ■ ■

On a beautiful summer morning in August 2000, Frank Smith of Gardner, Montana, a part-time Park Service employee, and his friend Pat Bents decided to hike to the top of Mount Norris in the game-rich Lamar Valley in northern Yellowstone National Park. The plan was to get an early start, but the men dawdled for a few hours, mesmerized by the rare and treasured appearance of three wolves playing on a low bench above the Lamar River.

By the time the men crossed the footbridge on the Lamar River Trail, it was early afternoon, so they decided to hike instead up to a long ridge below Mount Norris and study the massive mountain for a future ascent.

After two hours of brisk hiking, they stood on the ridge and looked down at the savanna-like landscape of the valley, with its herds of elk and bison contentedly grazing in scattered herds. Rather than return along the same path, the men decided to take a more direct route down a narrow draw between rock cliffs. The draw was well-timbered, and the shade would afford a welcome respite from the intense heat of the late summer sun.

"I was in the lead as we headed into the draw," Frank recalled later. "It didn't take long before we encountered lots of blowdown [fallen trees]. It was cooler in the draw, with a nice stream, but the brush and downed timber made it a real struggle. For every hundred feet we dropped in elevation, we had to zigzag two hundred feet around all the big trees lying across the draw.

"We were making lots of noise, talking loud, to alert a bear. Plus, I had a radiophone on my belt tuned to eleven park radio frequencies, and I had it cranked up all the way."

The men had just crawled over a massive red fir log and were contemplating the best route around another log jumble when a tremendous commotion erupted below them. "At first I thought we'd spooked some elk," Frank said, "then this loud huffing and woofing erupted, and I knew it was a bear. I was carrying a can of pepper spray in a holster on my hip, but Pat didn't have anything to protect himself, so he kinda stood behind me.

"That bear came so fast, I didn't have time to be scared. I was amazed by the intense amount of huffing sounds it was making. Thank God there was a lot of blowdown. It took me about three seconds to get the Velcro flap ripped open and the spray out. By then the bear was right in front of me.

"It happened like it was in slow motion, except my mind was working in overdrive. The bear hesitated about thirty feet away because of the big log between us. I'd read about how to use pepper spray, so I laid down a cloud of spray, expecting the bear to run into it and then run away. She ran through that big red cloud without blinking an eye!"

Instead of climbing over the big log, the bear charged to the left and came around the root wad. "At that point the grizzly was about seven feet away," Frank said. "I figured I'd really blast it this time and teach it a good lesson. As soon as the bear turned and started toward me I sprayed, and I sprayed, and I sprayed. I mean, I filled the whole draw with pepper spray, but it didn't seem to affect the bear at all."

The bear did skid to a halt, though, as if she were startled. She stood there for three or four seconds, then turned and ran about fifteen yards, into a thicket of brush below Pat.

Pat, defenseless and aware that Frank's spray can must be almost empty, feared the bear was circling and would charge from the other side. "She's circling around!" Pat yelled several times. "She's circling around!"

Then all was quiet for about ten seconds.

Suddenly the bear broke from the thicket and galloped downhill. "When I looked down, I got real nervous," Frank said. "There were bears moving everywhere! We'd walked into a sow with a bunch of big cubs. I didn't know what to do. I was almost out of pepper spray, and those young bears were almost as big as the sow."

To the relief of both men, the bears ran out of the draw and galloped away along a rock ledge. Frank and Pat hurried in the opposite direction and arrived safely back at the park visitor center.

Frank tried to figure out what had happened. "My guess," he said, "is that the loud noise of the spray coming out of the can, plus the realization that there were two of us, what with Pat being well over six feet tall, might have had something to do with the sow stopping. But she just didn't show any reaction to the pepper spray hitting her—no pawing at the air, no blinking eyes, no coughing or wheezing."

Much of the problem probably can be traced back to Frank's purchase of the spray. In the past, he had purchased a can of EPA-registered Counter Assault bear deterrent spray. Because the spray had just about reached its expiration date, he stopped at a sporting goods store in Billings, Montana, where they sold a different brand—a non-EPA-registered product. At the time, he was not aware of the importance of EPA registration. Because the unregistered spray was cheaper, he bought it.

"I'll never do that again," Frank said. "I guess I shouldn't complain, because the sow did stop her charge, but the pepper spray people claimed it knocks the heck out of a charging bear, and it didn't. I've read a lot about pepper spray since that attack, and I learned that not all pepper sprays are the same. I'm going to stick with UDAP or Counter Assault brands from now on."

Frank is not only a lover of nature but also a lover of bears, and he is still uncomfortable about the trauma he caused that sow. "I should have known better," he said. "A couple years earlier I was on a group nature hike. As we hiked down through a narrow draw, much like the one where I sprayed the bear, we kicked out a grizzly in a day bed. In retrospect, there were lots of open areas Pat and I could have hiked through that day. We just got hot and lazy.

"I lived through it, but I learned my lesson: buy only EPA-registered bear spray, and stay on the trails. If you bushwhack in grizzly country, you're tempting fate by walking into a bear's bedroom."

■ ■ ■

Wyoming resident Clark Turner is a big man with a big job. Standing six feet, four inches tall and weighing 240 pounds, he works for the U.S. Navy in the landlocked state of Wyoming. He's director of the Navy's strategic petroleum reserves in the oil-rich states of Utah, Colorado, and Wyoming.

There's another commodity that Wyoming is fast becoming known for—grizzly bears. Bears are being seen in areas where none were present for a century. It's proof that the great bear's protected status as a threatened species has helped it recover over the past three decades. But this has also created problems—for wildlife officials struggling with bear management and for folks who suddenly find their favorite hiking and hunting grounds inhabited by an animal that doesn't always run away.

Clark Turner's favorite hunting area, in the Teton Wilderness north of Jackson Lake in northwest Wyoming, was such a place. A decade ago, he never even thought about bear danger, but in recent years grizzly sightings had become more frequent—and troubling. The year before, Clark's hunting camp had been raided by a grizzly while the men were out hunting. Half an elk carcass, weighing about 250 pounds, had been dragged off. What kind of brute, Clark wondered, could pack off something that heavy?

But as he hiked into his favorite hunting area in the summer of 1998 to scout for bull moose in a swamp three miles away, he felt safe.

For one thing, there was very little bear sign. He'd hiked the trail in June and found lots of fresh bear sign, such as recent dung and overturned rocks where bears had been searching for grubs and ants, so he'd aborted the trip because he carried no means of defense against bears. But he had applied for a Wyoming moose permit and felt fortunate to have his application drawn out of a lottery for the area. He was anxious to get back there to scout for big bulls. Now, as he hiked along the trail, he was encouraged by the lack of bear sign. *They're probably all up in the high country by now,* he thought.

Clark had further reason to feel secure. He'd read an article about bear pepper spray in the *Bugle* magazine of the Rocky Mountain Elk Foundation and had been impressed by the testimonies of people who had stopped charging bears with the spray. He went to a sporting goods store to see about getting some for himself. Clark admitted to the clerk that he knew next to nothing about bear spray. Apparently neither did the salesman, but the man put on a good front.

The clerk assured Clark that the product he was selling was as good as anything else on the market, and he even went so far as to point out that it contained 10 percent oleoresin of capsicum. The spray was not an EPA-registered product, and Clark was ignorant of the fact the EPA considered the percentage of oleoresin of capsicum to be a misleading gauge of a spray's strength. Clark purchased the can of cheap and likely inferior spray, and now he strode confidently through the forest.

As Clark dropped into a low gully choked with dense brush and huge trees whose canopy dimmed the light below, he heard brush snapping. Then came furious huffing sounds from a thicket about thirty yards from the trail. He pulled out his bear spray, feeling a sense of relief to have it in his hands.

Seconds later a huge, dark-colored grizzly bear, silver mane bristling, burst out of the brush and lunged at him. Clark backed up, spraying as he went, but he was horrified to see the spray come out of the can in a weak, sputtering pattern.

The grizzly took a vicious swipe at his head, but Clark ducked and turned away. The hammerlike blow caught him on the left shoulder and sent him flying. Instantly the bear was upon him, tearing at his leg below the knee. The enraged bear then picked up all 240 pounds of Clark Turner and shook him violently.

Through all this pummeling, Clark kept spraying the bear until he emptied almost the entire can—with no apparent effect on the animal. Even as he was being ravaged by the bear, a frantic thought flashed through his mind: *Why isn't this stuff working?* The grizzly suddenly released Clark's leg and swung a paw at the can of spray. It missed but struck Clark's chest, smashing his binoculars and knocking the wind out of him.

Clark blacked out, right after getting the fleeting perception that the bear had stopped attacking him and was slowly retreating. Consciousness came back in fitful glimpses of his mangled leg, along with the startling recollection that he'd just been mauled by a grizzly.

For a few seconds, he lay heaving on the ground.

When he finally struggled to a sitting position, he was in for another shock. The boar grizzly stood just twenty-five feet away, staring at him. "My first thought was, 'This is it. I'm dead for sure, now.' But the bear turned and slowly walked away from me into the brush."

Though hurting in a hundred places, Clark tried to walk, but his injured leg was almost useless. Using a broken branch as a crutch, he hobbled away as best he could. His can of spray was almost empty, and his worst fear during the torturous trek back to his pickup was that the bear would follow him and renew the attack.

It was pure adrenaline and guts, and the will to survive, that drove Clark Turner to stumble in pain for the two miles back to his truck. It was there that he got another traumatic surprise: the pickup had a flat tire.

Bleeding, and slipping toward shock, he drove with the flat tire for several miles over a rough dirt road. By the time the pickup lurched onto the main highway, the flat tire on the rim was smoking badly. Clark waved frantically at motorists, but his disheveled, bloody appearance sent them careening around him. He was about to pass out when two paramedics returning from a training session stopped and rushed him to the hospital.

Wildlife officials hiked into the area to investigate. In the draw where Clark had been attacked, they discovered pieces of hide and bone from a calf moose. Clark Turner had been fortunate. He'd survived an attack from a grizzly guarding its food cache.

Most of Clark's injuries were superficial—cuts and bruises that would heal. The problem was his leg. Besides the outside wound, the bear had inflicted massive crushing injuries to the muscle. When he was released from the hospital two days later, the wound opened up and began discharging a pus-laced fluid. An antibiotic stopped the infection, but the flesh inside his leg had become necrotic; the tissue was dying. Unless something was done quickly, gangrene would set in. He could lose his leg. He could lose his life.

In these days of modern medical breakthroughs, there is still no miracle cure for this death of bodily tissue. Desperate doctors resorted to an archaic but tried-and-true method—the use of maggots. They're the same little white maggots that fill us with revulsion when we happen upon putrid garbage or a rotting carcass, for they feast on the dead. But the amazing thing about maggots is that they eat only dead flesh, not living tissue.

The doctors used maggots raised under sterile conditions in a laboratory. They inserted them into Clark's festering wound and covered the opening with a surgical mesh screen. For a month, Clark employed all his emotional resolve to ignore the squirming white grubs that had invaded his body and were consuming his dead flesh.

To the amazement of everyone but the doctors, the maggots dropped out of the wound when they had finished devouring the dead tissue, and Clark's leg quickly healed. He was left with a large crescent-shaped scar.

With the healing of his physical wounds came a burning anger over his plight. Why had this nightmare occurred? He'd been carrying pepper spray, but it hadn't stopped the bear. Why? Clark was shocked to discover that the spray he had purchased was an inferior product that not only did not have the amount of capsaicin necessary to stop the bear but also employed a propellant that lacked the pressure to fire the pepper airborne for more than a few feet.

Clark has now embarked upon a mission to educate the public about bear pepper sprays—the good stuff and the bad stuff. He has become an expert on the subject and speaks to outdoor groups about his experience and the need to carry an adequate, EPA-registered pepper spray.

Though he vilifies the inadequate pepper spray he carried that day, Clark insists it saved him from even worse injury. "That grizzly was eventually overcome by the red pepper," he said. "Why else would the bear leave me and then just stand there looking, then walk away?"

There is one comment that Clark hears too often about his attack: "Too bad you didn't have a gun to shoot the bear."

Clark shakes his head. "They don't understand. Unless you've been attacked by a grizzly at close quarters, you have no idea how fast they are, how fast they're on you, how quickly you're on the ground. If I had a gun, no way could I have brought it up and got a shot off."

In analyzing Clark Turner's case, the misleading sales pitch at the sporting goods store was at the root of his problem, which brings an urgency to the old adage: "Buyer beware!" The sputtering as the can released the spray was probably due to the propellant's inability to hold the heavy capsaicin without separating (possibly as a result of freezing). This imbalance, plus the lack of a more powerful propellant, combined to limit the spray's effective range to about six feet.

Though the label on the spray can claimed a 10 percent capsicum content, this is not a true indicator of a spray's hotness. But even in its tepid condition, the spray had the effect of lessening a potentially deadly encounter with a boar grizzly guarding his food cache—one of the most dangerous situations you can encounter with a grizzly.

■ ■ ■

The partial spray failures experienced by Frank Smith and Clark Turner might be shrugged off as the consequences of carrying inadequate, non-EPA-registered pepper spray in grizzly country. But don't try that argument with Matt Pelland. He's still in no mood, even after several years, to listen to someone question either his actions or his choice of pepper spray when he and his wife, Tracy, set out for a joyous hike up the Cracker Lake Trail in Glacier National Park on a sunny autumn morning in October 1998.

Matt and Tracy are nature lovers who yearned to break away from city life in their native state of Illinois. With the pluck and dogged determination of early-day pioneers, they struck out for the wilds of Montana.

They wanted wild, and they got it. Matt landed a job teaching on the Blackfeet Indian Reservation in the town of Browning, just half an hour's drive from Glacier National Park. For Tracy and Matt, it couldn't get any better than this. They fell in love with Glacier, awed by its spectacular peaks. So enraptured were they with this place that they were married in the fall of 1997 along the shores of Two Medicine Lake in the park.

Just about every weekend was spent hiking the trails of Glacier. The only problem was the hordes of vacationers who often crowded even the most remote trails and took away from the wilderness experience the Pellands sought. But tourist traffic dropped sharply after Labor Day, and by October the Pellands could reclaim many of the trails they had given over to the crowds.

Matt Pelland thought long and hard about pepper spray before that fateful October morning in 1998. He researched the subject and quickly realized that all bear pepper sprays were not alike. He chose an EPA-approved spray. No sense taking any chances in grizzly country.

It was a spectacular, sunny but cold day that greeted the Pellands as they strode up the Cracker Lake Trail. They wanted to get in one more long hike before snow buried the high country. The light was glorious, with its suffused amber glow settling upon every red-and-yellow-tinted bush. Most of all, they enjoyed the silence as they trudged up the normally crowded trail.

Five miles in, they came across fresh bear tracks, large and small, heading up the trail. They decided to continue. Tracy was in the lead when they entered a brushy stretch near a stream. They began yelling "Hey Bear! Hey Bear!" as they went.

Rounding a corner in the trail, Tracy looked up and gasped. A huge silver-furred grizzly stood in the trail about forty yards away. The bear spotted her and charged.

Tracy turned back and yelled, "Matt, it's a bear!" Matt frantically grabbed at the pepper spray, but he couldn't get it out of its hip holster. When Tracy glanced back, the bear was just twenty yards away and coming fast, low to the ground with ears laid back. Tracy was still ten yards from Matt when she sensed that the grizzly was about to pounce. She crouched down an instant before a thunderous blow sent her sprawling. The bear was on Tracy in a heartbeat, biting the back of her leg and shaking her.

Matt, still fumbling with the spray, ran twenty feet above the bear and yelled with arms waving to get it off Tracy. The bear jerked upright, spotted Matt, and leveled the 230-pound man like he was a toy. The bear then ripped at Matt's legs while he lay on his back. Finally the can of bear spray was in his hands, and he sprayed the bear full in the face. He sprayed and sprayed. And then he sprayed and sprayed some more from a distance not more than two feet. It had no visible effect on the bear.

Tracy, lying in a stunned heap twenty feet away, watched with detached fascination as the bear's head was engulfed in a red mist. Matt, almost out of spray, glanced over at Tracy and implored, "Run, Tracy! Run!"

Tracy lurched to her feet and started running back down the trail. The grizzly noticed her flight and left Matt to chase her. Tracy made it about forty yards before she felt a tremendous shove from behind pushing her face first into the muck of the trail.

Matt, bleeding and in shock, heard the *whump!* as the bear hit Tracy, heard her scream. He raised up to see the bear straddling his fallen wife. His analytical mind observed that the bear was doing more standing than savaging, and he had the feeling that the bear had spent its fury. For him to run forward waving his arms again would invite a fresh wave of rage from the bear. His wife needed help that he could not provide. He then made the most difficult decision of his life. He turned and ran for help. He stumbled downhill to a stream a hundred feet below the trail and staggered along its banks toward the trailhead.

Tracy, a registered nurse, had seen disfiguring facial injuries from car accidents, and now, with 400 pounds of angry bear straddling her, the thought flashed through her mind that she must keep the bear from biting her face. She curled into a fetal position on her knees. The bear bit the back of her head, her back, her legs. Then it bit into her side and violently shook her, but she was wearing three layers of heavy shirts, so the bear's teeth did not penetrate her body.

Tracy recalls that the bear played with her like a cat would with a mouse, pawing at her, trying to turn her face up, but whenever the bruin knocked her over, she quickly assumed a face-down position. Yet even during the trauma of the attack, the thought,

This bear is not going away, but it's really not hurting me, either, flashed through Tracy's mind.

And then the bear did the unthinkable. It laid down on Tracy, squashing her body into the muddy trail. She suffered the tremendous weight on top of her in silence, never moving, barely breathing. Oddly, while the bear was atop her, she could smell the pungent aroma of red pepper on its fur.

Tracy said the bear probably laid on her for just a few seconds, but it seemed like an eternity. It was the most difficult part of the entire attack—to just lie there under the sow's body. With a loud groan, the bear lifted its weight off her. The bear straddled her again, clamped down on her head with its jaws and partially lifted her up, then released its grip. She dropped back to a fetal position, waiting for the next assault.

Silence. In her ravaged condition, she could not comprehend the passing of time. Twice she blacked out. With the numbness wearing off and pain increasing, she dared to lift her head. The bear was gone. So was Matt. Was he still alive? Could she administer first aid and save his life? Or was he dead, dragged off by the bear into a dense thicket nearby?

She knew she had to get away from the area quickly, but she had no idea in which direction the bear had gone, so she too scrambled through the brush for the safety of the creek below. "The brush was very thick near the creek," Tracy recalled. "I had to push and roll over it to get into the water."

She knew shock would set in soon, so she gulped down some water and took four Advil tablets for the pain that was now shooting through her body. Fearful that the bear might come back for her, in the ice-cold water she washed the blood from her body and clothes.

She stayed in the stream for a long time, hoping to keep the bear from following her scent. After a mile she was soaked and near hypothermic from the frigid waters. When the trail intersected the stream, she left the water and hurried down the path.

"It was the most horrible part of the whole ordeal, not knowing if Matt was dead or alive," she said.

Matt was suffering through the same agony back at Swiftcurrent Inn, fearing for his wife, while he alerted park rangers. The rangers were responsive, but it seemed to Matt that they took a long time getting started up the trail to Tracy.

The rescuers were preparing to leave when they spotted a bedraggled woman stumbling onto the trailhead parking lot. Tracy saw the rangers and was about to blurt out a plea to them to go back and find her husband, when she saw Matt. "The moment I saw Matt, I burst into tears," Tracy said, emotion still evident in her tone years later.

"I must have had some pepper spray on my eyelashes because it mixed with the tears and then burned my eyes. *Now it works!* I remember thinking. The only place the pepper could have come from was from the bear's fur."

Tracy and Matt were taken to the hospital in Browning and released. Tracy's injuries were mostly superficial, but she did have nine puncture wounds and tears that required stitches. The bear never did mark her face. Matt's leg was torn badly, but it healed quickly, with no complications.

Rangers returned to the attack site and soon spotted the bear. She was a beautiful blond sow with two cubs. As they watched her, she dug a marmot from its burrow and gulped it down without sharing a morsel with her cubs. The Park Service allows some leeway in its policy toward bears that attack humans. If a bear attacks a human as an instinctive reaction of self-defense and does not feed on the human, but immediately retreats, that bear may be allowed to live. Rangers decided to spare the life of this bear.

The Pellands' physical injuries healed quickly; not so the emotional damage. They weren't as quick to take long hikes, sometimes opting for a car trip through the park instead of a hike along a trail. They have slowly returned to the trails they loved so much, but now they're a lot more cautious. They stay away from trails where dense brush grows, and they always try to hike with others, even tourists.

Matt said that, while he's certainly not glad they were attacked, he has seen some positive results grow from the experience. He and Tracy have grown closer as husband and wife. They don't take things, even little ones, for granted anymore. Their woods sense, and sense of awareness, is a lot keener when they take to the wilderness.

Tracy remains upbeat and is largely over the trauma, but Matt has not been able to accept the failure of the bear pepper spray. And he is still angry that he was forced to make that agonizing decision to leave his beloved wife with the bear, just because the spray had failed to send the bear running away.

The problem wasn't a mechanical malfunction with the can. Matt said the bear's head was turned orange by the spray, and Tracy added that she looked over and saw the bear's head engulfed in a red mist as Matt was spraying. Both Tracy and Matt could smell the red pepper in the air.

Other hikers had stopped charging bears in their tracks with a lot less spraying by using the same product. Why hadn't their can of spray done its job?

There has been a lot of conjecture about why an EPA-registered bear-deterrent spray failed. Armchair experts pointed out that Matt was slow in getting the pepper spray out and that Tracy ran from the bear not once but twice. Bristling, Matt counters that those critics weren't there. They weren't faced with the sudden thunderous rush of a berserk animal on a sunny afternoon hike. They weren't under the bear, at its mercy. They didn't have the hysterical thought Matt had when he sprayed and sprayed at the bear's head only a couple of feet away: *Oh my god, this stuff isn't working!*

There you have it: an EPA-registered pepper spray that failed to stop an attacking grizzly bear, resulting in injuries to both Tracy and Matt Pelland. And yet, even in the face of this apparent failure, some grizzly experts find positive aspects to this incident.

A quick analysis sheds some light on their optimism. Though Matt Pelland was not able to get his spray out in time to stop the bear's initial attack, his subsequent spraying seems to have lessened the bear's aggression. His spray did not make the bear flee, but the animal's lethargic actions afterward lend credence to the hypothesis that the bear was indeed suffering, even through its instinctive defensive rage. Bears that have had their way with humans have inflicted horrible damage, often sending victims to the hospital for months, but the Pellands' injuries were relatively light.

The most curious aspect of this incident is the odd behavior of the grizzly, supposedly in a fit of rage, suddenly lying on its victim. I contacted two experts on grizzly bear attacks—Stephen Herrero and Barry Gilbert—for their take on the strange encounter.

Herrero concluded that the bear laid down on Tracy because it was finally overcome, after a long delay, by the heavy dose of pepper it had absorbed. Gilbert also concluded that the bear, overcome by the pepper spray, simply could not continue the attack and had to lie down. He said the sow's listless grasping of Tracy's head, and the fact that the bear released her head before leaving, made it clear this was not a typical tearing, slashing attack by an enraged bear.

Gilbert summed up the Pellands' attack: "The sow grizzly had her way with Matt Pelland once and Tracy Pelland twice, yet they were treated and released from the hospital that day. That sounds to me like the spray did its job. I think we sometimes have unreasonable expectations about pepper spray. It's a bear deterrent, meaning it deters an attack. That doesn't necessarily mean it stops it. It just means it lessens the damage and makes the bear move off. It's great when we hear about a charging grizzly that's stopped in its tracks by pepper spray, but we have to remember that it's unreasonable, and it's dangerous, to expect bear spray to accomplish that every time."

Gilbert, who was himself attacked years earlier by a sow grizzly that he stumbled upon while doing research in Yellowstone, is more perturbed by the armchair experts who chose to dissect the attack on the Pellands and find fault in the young couple's actions. "Unless you've been attacked by a grizzly, you have no idea how fast, how big they are when they come at you.

"In my attack, that bear was already in midair, launching herself at me before I could react. It really angered me, while I was lying in a hospital bed with almost a thousand stitches, to have my colleagues dissecting my actions with a detached indifference, as if the attack were my fault, insinuating that it would have ended differently if I hadn't turned and started to run. But they weren't there. They don't know what it was like to see that bear launching herself at me."

■ ■ ■

If there is any good news in this chapter on bear–spray failures, it is the fact that ten of the twelve spray-failure incidents I investigated involved cheap spray, often water-based. Thanks to the EPA's vigilant efforts to register bear-deterrent sprays and enforce uniform standards—plus efforts of the Interagency Grizzly Bear Committee and the Center for Wildlife Information to educate the public on spray contents and proper use—these inferior products are seen less and less on shelves as store managers and consumers become more knowledgeable.

Also of great importance is the fact that even the inadequate pepper sprays had the effect, in most cases, of lessening the damage and eventually forcing the bear to abort its attack because of the cumulative effects of the red pepper. For that reason, these incidents are viewed as only partial failures because they did reduce the severity of the attack.

The EPA-registered bear-deterrent pepper spray that the Pellands used, while not stopping the bear initially, eventually forced the bear to move off. But the fact remains that it was an EPA-registered pepper spray. Why didn't it immediately stop the bear? In forthcoming chapters, there will be many thrilling accounts of folks stopping charging bears in their tracks using EPA-registered pepper sprays. Why not the Pellands?

That question may never be fully answered. However, it would help to harken back to the summation in the previous chapter of Stephen Herrero's survey of pepper spray incidents. He learned that some bears seem to have a higher tolerance to pepper spray than most other bears.

Chuck Jonkel, who pioneered the development of pepper spray as a bear deterrent, noticed the same thing while testing red pepper on captive bears. Not all bears reacted the same way.

Both bears and humans vary greatly in their responses to pain. Most retreat when it hurts too much. But a few people—and you can see this while watching the Friday night fights on television—react to pain with increased fury, until they are either subdued or victorious.

A small percentage of bears also react to an increase in pain with an increase in rage. It's another good reason to avoid the dangerous thinking that pepper spray is security in a can: when a grizzly bursts out of the brush in full charge forty yards away, security is past tense.

CHAPTER 6

Tougher Than a Speeding Bullet

oday's high-powered rifle is capable of delivering a heavy lead bullet encased in a copper jacket at velocities approaching three thousand feet per second. But this dubious miracle of modern technology saves the best for last. Packing hundreds of foot-pounds of pent-up energy, the heavy slug arrives with the subtlety of a cruise missile, reducing living flesh in its path to a pulverized, atomized, homogenized mass of sliced, diced, tenderized bloody gel, and hard bone to a jumble of tiny white shards.

The big cats—leopard, tiger, lion—terrible and lethal in their own right, are easily felled by a well-placed bullet. Even the great pachyderms plow a deep furrow in the African savanna when hit with a .375 H&H magnum.

But against a charging grizzly, it's not enough. No doubt harking back to its behavior during the Pleistocene epoch, a grizzly's rage increases when injured. It's a disturbing fact for a gun owner to accept: a salvo of hot lead smashing into a charging grizzly just tends to spur it on toward the source of its pain.

More often than not, the grizzly has gained its fierce reputation when it was dead on its feet, having already been shot through and through. Yet to the shock, the horror, and occasionally the demise of the shooter, the great bear kept coming—its heart shot to pieces, its lungs blown out—until bear or man, or both, found their final peace.

Bear number 34 was such a grizzly. He was a bad bear, and he needed to be killed before he killed someone. At 670 pounds of taut muscle, the big grizzly was a berserk, rage-filled beast that had been killing cattle on a ranch near Dubois, Wyoming, in the summer of 1994.

Like Charles Manson, his psychotic human counterpart, bear 34 didn't become a killer overnight. It took years of pain and suffering to produce something so horrible.

The story of bear 34 actually began twenty-two years earlier when a beautiful young male grizzly bear with a lustrous charcoal-colored coat was live-trapped near Dubois. Biologists fastened an ear tag—number 34. They also fitted the bear with a radio collar.

To avoid damaging a bear's neck, these radio collars are connected with a canvas band that rots away after a few years, allowing the collar to drop off. But something went terribly wrong. Long after the radio had stopped transmitting, the collar stayed snapped around bear 34's neck.

Like all male grizzlies, the young bear's neck grew thick with muscles, but the collar stayed fastened around his neck like a garrote. First it cut through the bear's hide, then into his neck muscles, where it grated against festering flesh and squeezed his upper neck so severely that the nerves near the ears were permanently damaged, rendering him deaf and near-mad with pain. And when a grizzly feels pain, rage is a by-product.

Bear 34 was live-trapped again near the Diamond G Ranch in 1992, and it was then that state biologists discovered the old radio collar embedded in his neck. One can only guess at the fury that bear 34 must have felt, tranquilized and conscious but unable to move while he again endured excruciating pain at the hands of men while the radio collar was finally removed.

The next year, bear 34 became a cattle killer on the Diamond G Ranch, as did two other grizzlies. One of the grizzlies disappeared, and the other one was euthanized, but bear 34 was caught and released several miles from the ranch because he was a study bear.

With teeth worn down, his neck wound still festering, and his food source of cattle removed, bear 34 roamed the remote black timber forests of the Bridger–Teton National Forest near Jackson, Wyoming, in a rage—a 700-pound time bomb waiting to explode.

Clayton Peterson is a no-nonsense Westerner, tough and straightforward as a Wyoming winter. He loves to hunt elk, but in recent years he and other hunters found their pursuit of elk near the game-rich Davis Hill country disrupted by the growing presence of grizzly bears. There had already been a few incidents involving bears and humans, and many hunters had quit coming to the area, but Clay loved the high alpine summits and black timber pockets.

Clay knew that the longer he hunted there, the greater his chances were of encountering a grizzly. He purchased a .375 H&H magnum rifle. It was much bigger than he needed for elk hunting, but Clay wanted the security of the big gun just in case he ran into a cranky bear.

On a frosty, late September morning in 1994, Clay moved stealthily along a low ridge in a dense stand of black timber near Davis Hill. As he crossed a small draw littered with fallen trees, Clay eased over a log and caught movement out of the corner of his eye. A large, dark-colored bear about sixty yards away was moving toward him. He raised his rifle but hesitated, thinking it was just a big black bear. The bear disappeared behind a screen of trees, and he guessed it caught his human scent and scampered off. Suddenly the bear's head popped up above a log just ten feet away. One look at the bear's face and he realized it was a grizzly. Although Clay didn't know it at the time, this was not just any grizzly. It was bear 34.

The next instant the bear lunged at Clay, and Clay blasted him, sending a bullet into the grizzly's hump. The 200-grain slug disintegrated upon impact with the bear's spine, sending hot lead fragments ripping through both lungs. The remainder of the bullet traveled along the underside of the bear's spine, tearing away the main aorta. For all practical purposes, bear 34 was dead on his feet. He was also pissed off.

The grizzly lunged as Clay frantically worked the gun's bolt. The bear's teeth clamped down on Clay's arm, snapping the bone at the elbow. The bear picked him up and shook him violently, then threw him over a blown-down tree.

Bear 34 then staggered backward, but he came looking for Clay Peterson once again. Though stunned and in pain, Clay was able to chamber another shell but inadvertently flipped on the safety. He squeezed the trigger hard enough to bend it, but nothing happened.

The massive grizzly swung a vicious paw one last time at Clay Peterson. The four-inch claws ripped Clay's face away, sending him flying backward. Blinded by his own blood, Clay pulled out his .44 magnum pistol but could not find the bear.

Clay lay in shock for several seconds. He didn't know if the bear was nearby and bent on finishing the job. He gingerly touched his face. It was gone. Hanging by a large flap of skin was his dislodged nose and an eyeball. And blood was pouring everywhere. He gingerly took the face flap and laid it back into place, allowing him to see somewhat out of one eye.

He knew the country well and stumbled down a ridge to find his brother-in-law, the man with whom he had gone hunting. When the brother-in-law saw Clay, he almost fainted. When they arrived at their tethered horses, Clay's faithful horse, seeing the bloody, disfigured person approaching, went berserk and refused to allow him to mount. A helicopter was called in, and Clay was flown to the hospital in Jackson.

Authorities found bear 34 dead a few hundred yards from the attack scene. For the big grizzly, the pain was finally gone. A necropsy confirmed the damage from the radio collar, including the bear's deafness.

But the assault on Clay Peterson was not over. While lying in a hospital bed, an agent for the U.S. Fish and Wildlife Service interviewed Clay, refusing to accept his story about the attack and attempting to cajole him into admitting he had somehow gotten between a sow and her cubs. Clay, still fuming during our inter-view as he recalled the conversation, said, "The guy was trying to talk me into admitting that it was all my fault, that no grizzly would purposely attack a human. If I could have somehow got out of that hospital bed, I'd have decked him."

Later, Clay was visited by a more tactful officer from the Wyoming Fish and Game Department. When Clay described the bear, he noticed the officer's eyes register recognition. Clay became suspicious and began investigating. It was then that he discovered the dreadful history behind bear 34.

Clay has mended well, considering the tremendous damage inflicted by a virtually dead bear. Surgeons were able to reattach his face, using part of his hip to rebuild his nose. They were also able to save his eye, though the nerves in the eyelid were damaged beyond repair and he now has to sleep with one eye open. Medical costs exceeded $158,000.

Though Clay harbors no animosity toward grizzly bears, and especially the unfortunate animal that attacked him, he remains bitter toward the Fish and Wildlife Service and the state of Wyoming for allowing such a bear to be injured and then protected.

Clay Peterson is also adamant that it won't happen again. Next time a grizzly comes after him, he'll be ready. He's adopted a bigger, more sturdy bullet that he believes will surely get the job done.

■ ■ ■

Fred Woods raises his eyebrows at this philosophy of increased firepower to stop a bear. He went after a bear with a bigger bullet, even a bigger gun. It didn't help. Fred is the host of the Portland, Oregon, sportsman's television program *Northwest Hunter*. Fred's choice of caliber for a brown-bear (grizzly) hunting trip to Alaska was the .416 Remington magnum. It's an elephant gun whose 400-grain bullet and case resemble a small mortar. And yet it wasn't enough.

One morning, Fred spotted a big brown bear and moved to within two hundred yards before carefully placing the crosshairs of his scope on the bear's shoulder. The big gun roared, and the bear dropped. Fred jumped up, exulting in his quick kill. But the bear struggled to its feet, spotted him, and charged. Fred rammed another bullet into the chamber and took careful aim at the chest of the oncoming bear. The bullet literally knocked the bear backward, and it landed in a heap, where it lay heaving its last breaths.

Fred thought, *Whew, that was close!* As a precaution, he chambered the last bullet. When he looked up, he was startled to see the bear back on its feet, coming at him again.

Fred's third shot knocked the big bear sideways but didn't put it down. The bear, now less than a hundred yards away, hobbled toward him on three legs. Fred frantically grabbed for extra shells from his pockets and shoved them into the rifle's magazine. He threw up his gun and fired again when the bear was sixty yards away. This time he heard the loud *splat!* as the heavy slug pulverized the bear's chest.

But the bear didn't go down. As Fred hastily rammed the next bullet into the chamber, he thought, *Two more shots, and then this bear's gonna be on me.*

The bear was thirty yards away when the next slug smashed into its chest, sending forth a crimson plume of blood and gore. The bear went down, but as Fred rammed his last bullet into the rifle's chamber, he had no more illusions that it was over. He brought the rifle to his shoulder as 800 pounds of pulverized brown bear struggled to its feet and lurched forward to fulfill its death wish.

Fred looked through his scope at the bear's eyes, filled with rage and pain. He had one last bullet. When the concussion of the blast echoed through the barren hills, the bear nose-dived into the earth less than ten feet from Fred Woods.

Realizing he'd been fortunate that the bear's charge had begun far enough away that he could get off six shots, Fred began investigating bear pepper spray as an alternative, just in case a grizzly should jump out of the brush at close range. Fred told me, "I knew from personal experience that if you don't kill a bear immediately, shooting it some more only increases its rage. I chose pepper spray because I became convinced that it canceled that rage factor."

Fred drew a few chuckles and smirks when he strapped on a can of bear pepper spray on the first day of an Alaska guided hunt for caribou in the fall of 1999. That afternoon, Fred and another hunter, plus the guide, went on a scouting trip. Four hours later, Fred was in the lead as the men returned to their camp. As they came around the front of the first tent, a brown bear cub ran away squealing. A huge brown bear sow exploded out of a tent thirty feet away and charged them. While the other men frantically struggled to get their rifles off their shoulders, Fred pulled out his bear pepper spray and gave the sow a full blast at twenty feet. The bear skidded to a halt, pawing at the air, then swapped ends and galloped away with her cub close behind.

"A guy with a big game rifle is actually handicapped if he's suddenly charged," Fred said. "These guns have to be free of dirt and snow, so most hunters keep them on a sling over a shoulder. No way can you get that gun off your shoulder, chamber a shell, and then make a killing shot at a bear barreling at you through the brush."

A cadre of outdoors people who recognize the logistical nightmare of unslinging a rifle and then trying to find a charging grizzly in the crosshairs of a scope have opted for a sidearm, namely the .44 magnum pistol. Fred Woods snorts at such logic.

"The old-timers in Alaska tell those people that if they're gonna use a .44 mag for self-defense against a brown bear, they should file down the front sight. When the nimrod asks why, the old-timer tells him, 'That way when the bear takes it from you and shoves it up your ass, it won't hurt so much.'"

Besides the obvious ballistic inadequacy of a pistol, the fact remains that very few people can shoot one accurately. At a gathering of outfitters and guides in Wyoming, a state official hooked up a black-bear decoy to his all-terrain vehicle, using a hundred feet of rope. Six guides, experienced in pistol shooting, emptied their sidearms as the decoy was pulled by at thirty yards. Out of thirty-six shots, one bullet struck the black bear—in the rear paw! The nervous driver was overheard swearing, "And I thought that was the wind whistling past my ears!" No doubt another section of rope was added on subsequent exercises.

■ ■ ■

Wyoming resident Pat Van Vleet realized he needed something for self-defense when he started seeing grizzly sign in his favorite hunting area in the Bridger–Teton National Forest in 1993. At first it was just sign, such as huge bear tracks in the mud and massive claw marks on trees. In 1994 he saw his first grizzly, a sow with cub that spotted him at seventy-five yards and ran away.

The increasing amount of bear sign changed the way Pat and his dad, Ken, hunted the vast series of drainages. They no longer felt free to hike for miles in the dark to get to a secluded meadow where the elk were rutting. And they became very careful about leaving food in camp. They hoped these precautions would reduce their chances of encountering a grizzly. They didn't.

An incident on an elk-scouting trip into Grizzly Creek in the fall of 1997 brought the situation to a head. As Pat and his dad entered a dark draw choked with blown-down spruce and Douglas fir trees, they heard shuffling and pawing ahead. They weren't sure if it was an elk, so they eased forward until they stood in the heart of the blowdown, yet no elk was visible.

Suddenly a huge brown grizzly boar stood up and stared at them from less than fifty yards away. Pat's dad had the rifle up, crosshairs on the tiny white star on the bear's chest. For five minutes, the grizzly and the two men stared each other down in silence. The bear slowly dropped down and walked away, occasionally throwing a glance back at them. The bear had not charged, nor had he acted aggressively, but neither was he afraid of them.

Pat's dad was adamant. From now on, one of them would carry a shotgun loaded with rifled slugs. They tried that tack a few times, but it meant one of them could not hunt with bow or rifle, so Pat investigated bear pepper spray as a defense against bears. He visited a sporting goods store, unsure of what he needed and totally ignorant of the importance of knowing. A salesman shoved a can of cheap pepper spray into his hands and told him all pepper sprays were the same.

The next fall, Pat and his dad bowhunted in the area, but the presence of so much grizzly sign, plus a few unnerving nights in camp when they smelled the powerful stench of a bear nearby, convinced Pat's dad that they should leave the area rather than chance a bear encounter.

On September 27, Pat, his dad, his uncle, and another man, E. J. Steigelweir, traveled into Grizzly Creek to set up camp the day before elk rifle season. Pat's dad was edgy. Bear sign was everywhere. Huge logs were turned over, and bear scat littered every trail. Either there was a very busy grizzly nearby, or there were a lot of bears in the area. Only later did they learn that biologists estimated that up to seventeen grizzlies had descended upon Grizzly Creek and other side drainages.

That evening Pat and his dad rode an all-terrain vehicle (ATV) in as far as they could go, then hiked for almost an hour to the top of Black Rock Creek to scout for elk. There was a lot of fresh elk sign, so they decided to hunt there next morning. On the way back to camp a blizzard set in, dumping six inches of wet snow before the sky cleared and the temperature dropped below freezing.

The next morning the four men drove their ATVs to the end of the trail in the dark. The two older men planned to hunt the elk herd from the bottom of the Black Rock drainage while Pat and E. J. hiked to the top to watch the large meadows below in case the elk came up.

Pat recalled, "Dad was really freaking out. He had this bad feeling about us sneaking through the dark. He wanted us to wait until daylight, but we wanted to be up on top at first shooting light."

Pat and E. J. made it to the top of Black Rock Creek in plenty of time to set up before dawn. The meadow below was empty, so Pat bugled, making a sound like the mating call of a bull elk. Four bugles erupted from a half mile below, but a narrow finger of timber blocked their view of one corner of the meadow. Pat decided to move down to it. That way, E. J. could watch the main meadow and Pat could keep an eye on the other opening.

Pat eased down the slope about a hundred yards, then sneaked along the finger of timber to a small rise, where he sat on a large log that afforded him a view for three hundred yards below. After five minutes, he took off his fanny pack and began munching on a candy bar.

Some animals trotted into the open area below, and Pat cranked up his scope to nine power. He was trying to find the animals in the scope when he heard a shuffling sound behind him. His first thought was, *Wow! The elk are right behind me.*

When he turned around he saw fur—brown, grizzled fur. A sow and two cubs were nosing along the log just twenty-five yards away. His heart felt like a giant fist was squeezing it. *Maybe they won't notice me,* he thought. As he lowered the rifle, a cub spotted him and began squealing. The sow instantly charged.

Pat recalled, "I grabbed the pepper spray and sprayed the sow when she was fifteen feet away, but the stuff just sputtered out of the can in a thin stream, maybe ten feet. The sow hesitated, and I sprayed at her again, then she just barreled through the cloud. I was out of spray by then, so I turned and ran. It was an impulsive thing."

The sow bit Pat's left ankle, sending him sprawling, then bit into his right arm. Pat curled into a fetal position. The sow swatted him and lunged for his head, but he tucked it down.

The sow then bit into his right side and shook him hard before flinging him to the ground and biting into his stomach. Fortunately, Pat's heavy hunting coat took the brunt of the bear's powerful jaws. The bear literally pulled him to his feet before furiously shaking him again and throwing him down. Pat hit the ground hard, with the bear right on top of him again, slashing and tearing.

"I was getting knocked around pretty good," Pat said. "Then the bear suddenly leaps straight into the air, bellowing and biting and pawing at the air. Then I heard a loud *whop!* and the bear pitched over backwards."

Pat didn't know what was going on, but at least the bear wasn't on him anymore. As he scrambled away, he thought, *All that, and I only got a sprained ankle.*

"Then I brought up my right hand," Pat said, "and saw a big hole through the palm, and I looked at my ankle and saw the bone sticking out. I was finding bite marks and tears on every part of my body. But when I looked down at my belly and saw the blood, that was too much. I didn't know whether the bear had torn my guts out. It was horrible working my fingers under my coat, feeling my belly. The muscle was torn, but my intestines were still inside. "

As shock set in, Pat's knees buckled and he crumpled to the ground. Crimson fingers of blood slowly spread out from his ravaged body. And then a worried voice called out, "Are you all right?" It was E. J.

E. J. had heard and saw a far different version of the attack than Pat, who thought the attack had lasted only a few seconds. E. J. had come running when he heard the commotion below, then heard Pat yell, "She's gonna get me! She's gonna get me! Get her off me!" As E. J. ran downhill, he saw Pat and the sow in a desperate struggle, with Pat punching and kicking at the bear.

E. J. was frantic. He had to stop the bear, but he didn't want to shoot his friend. When he first found the bear in his scope, the animal had just pulled Pat upright, and he dared not shoot, but after the bear threw Pat down and started in on him again, E. J. squeezed the trigger, then shot the sow again as she whirled above his fallen friend, madly pawing the air.

There was no reason for Pat's dad to be suspicious about the two shots that came from above, but some inner voice told him his son was in trouble. Five minutes later when Pat's dad and his uncle arrived, they found Pat in a desperate condition, lying in an ever-widening pool of blood. It appeared that every part of his body was bitten, torn, bloody.

Pat's dad sank to the ground, wringing his hands in anguish. He's a tough man not prone to tears, but as he watched his son moaning in agony, he began to weep. Their situation was desperate. They faced a long, difficult hike down to the four-wheelers, then a one-hour ride along a rough trail back to the pickups, which were parked an hour's drive from a paved road.

Pat's dad had accidentally brought along a cell phone, but he doubted it would get any response in the middle of nowhere. He threw the phone to E. J. and ordered him to race to the top of the divide and call for help. The younger man ran for forty yards, then stopped and yelled back, "What should I tell them?"

"Tell them there's a man up here bleeding to death!"

For an hour Pat lay in the snow, and hypothermia began to set in. His skin turned blue and his teeth chattered uncontrollably as his dad and uncle worked in vain to start a fire in the wet snow.

And then they heard the *whop-whop-whop* of a helicopter echoing off the mountains above.

E. J. had been able to contact a 911 operator in Idaho, who transferred his call to a 911 operator in Wyoming. When the helicopter pilot spotted the red snow, he banked the craft and executed a tight landing just one hundred yards away and Pat was evacuated to a hospital.

Doctors worked feverishly on Pat in the emergency room. In addition to his obvious wounds, they also discovered that his left shoulder and right hip were dislocated. He was in the hospital for eight days. On the second day, Pat received a phone call from someone who wanted to talk to him about pepper spray. Unable to hold the phone in his bandaged hands, and seething over the inadequacy of the spray he had used, he had his wife bring the receiver to his ear, intending to give the guy a good piece of his mind.

The man on the other end of the line was Mark Matheny, owner of Universal Defense Alternative Products, maker of UDAP Pepper Power. Mark told Pat that he also had been attacked by a grizzly and assured Pat that his wounds would heal. Despite his resolve to the contrary, Pat found himself responding to the sensitive approach of a stranger who had endured a similar nightmare. Before Mark hung up, he promised to send some of his UDAP Pepper Power to Pat's house.

When Pat arrived home, the box containing several cans of pepper spray was sitting on his front porch in a FedEx overnight delivery box. A week later, while Pat waited for a friend to take him to the hospital for physical therapy, he picked up a can of the UDAP spray and limped out to his back deck, still dubious at that point about all pepper sprays.

He flipped off the safety and pressed the trigger. He was startled by the loud, intense blast of red pepper. "That stuff must have shot out fifty feet," Pat said. "This was the stuff I should have had against that bear."

Then a slight breeze brought the orange cloud drifting back to Pat's face. He howled in pain and was instantly blinded. When his friend arrived ten minutes later, he thought Pat had gone mad. He found Pat thrashing around in the bathtub, bandages soaked and drooping, working desperately to get the hot pepper off his burning skin.

Pat and Mark Matheny became friends over the phone, and

it was then Pat learned that all pepper sprays aren't the same. Rather than lament his ordeal, Pat stepped forward to become a vocal proponent of EPA-listed pepper spray, often speaking at sportsman's meetings and Boy Scout camps.

To those who wonder if he would have been better off shooting the grizzly, Pat adamantly replies, "No way could I have shot that bear. She came so fast, I wouldn't have had time to find her in the scope. I would've just wounded her and made her even madder than she was."

Pat recovered and is back on the job driving a truck for UPS. His left shoulder is still sore and probably won't get any better. But Pat has turned even that into a positive. He says it reminds him how fortunate he was, and how much worse it could have been.

■ ■ ■

There have been instances in which a gun has stopped a charging grizzly. But even those success stories can be tainted by the guilt some shooters feel after wasting the life of such a magnificent beast. And when it involves a sow, the tragedy is increased because the cubs are usually too young to survive alone. EPA-registered bear pepper spray could have accomplished the same results for the person being attacked but would have allowed the bears to live.

Several conservation groups, concerned with the needless killing of grizzly bears by hunters who are defending themselves, have petitioned those states surrounding Yellowstone National Park to require hunters to carry bear pepper spray. In 2000, thirty-two grizzly bears died in the Yellowstone ecosystem.

Twenty-three of those deaths were caused by humans, and at least eleven were due to conflicts with hunters.

"The hunter issue is popping up as the primary cause of grizzly bear mortality in the greater Yellowstone ecosystem for the past several years now," said Sierra Club spokeswoman Louisa Wilcox in an interview with the *Missoulian* newspaper. "I think this is certainly cause for alarm."

Many people who respect the bear believe it's time for sportsmen who hunt near Glacier and Yellowstone National Parks in the states of Idaho, Montana, and Wyoming to step forward and make a conservation statement by publicly advocating pepper spray as an alternative defense against bears. There's even a catchy slogan ready-made by bear spray enthusiasts: "Spray 'em, don't slay 'em!"

CHAPTER 7

Hunting Guides and Bears

Generally, a hunting guide's biggest concern is getting the client within range of a trophy big game animal. Not so with Gary Clutter. He took his guiding job a lot more seriously, especially in grizzly country. And especially after fellow guide Joe Heimer's nightmare hunt the year before.

Joe had led his client Sonja Crowley along a ridge just north of Yellowstone National Park on a late November morning. The grizzlies should have been hibernating by then, but a warm Chinook wind had blown in, melting much of the snow that covered the bears' dens. Joe told me that he was helping Sonja by carrying her rifle when he topped a small knoll and spotted a grizzly feeding in the snow just sixty feet away. Thinking it was a young boar, Joe and Sonja slowly retreated behind a tree about a hundred feet away, expecting the bear to move off.

They were startled when three small cubs ambled into the opening in front of them. A split second later the sow, having caught their scent, was in full charge, head low, ears laid back. Joe snapped Sonja's rifle to his shoulder and fired but missed. The sow leveled him with a hard blow to the shoulder, then bit him above the right knee and left leg.

Sonja rushed forward to retrieve her rifle and help Joe, but the sow saw her and gave chase as she fled. The bear walloped her in the back, then took her face into its jaws and violently shook her. The bear suddenly broke off the attack and ran back to the cubs.

Joe struggled to his feet, grabbed Sonja's rifle, and started toward the fallen woman, but the sow came at him again. This time Joe blasted the bear and it dropped. When he got to Sonja, he gasped. The left side of her face was gone, and she was bleeding profusely. Joe was helping her lay the torn flesh back into place when a huge bellow ripped through the air close behind him. Joe whirled and had just enough time to point the barrel of the gun at the enraged bear's face before he fired. The slug hit the bear between the eyes, killing it instantly, and the animal slid to a halt under his feet.

In the aftermath of the attack, Joe Heimer healed quickly, but for his client, it was much more serious. Sonja Crowley required extensive surgery and lost most of the sight in her left eye. Medical costs reached two hundred thousand dollars.

Gary Clutter wasn't going to allow that to happen to him or his clients. Like most hunting guides, he didn't carry a rifle, but he was not defenseless; he had purchased a can of Frontiersman bear spray. And as a fire department captain in Bozeman, Montana, Gary was well aware of the potency of pepper spray in police work.

He also knew for a fact that the stuff worked on bears. Shortly after he'd moved into a rural area, a 130-pound black bear became a daily raider at a backyard bird feeder. After the bear damaged the feeder and an apple tree, Gary spotted it and chased it up a tree. With the bear staring at him from ten feet above, Gary sprayed it full in the face. The bear fell from the tree and ran away, bawling and swiping at its face. It then ran full speed into a red fir tree. The groggy bruin staggered across the road and dug a hole in the mud of a marsh, moaning and crying for almost an hour. Though the bear visited other residents after that, it never ventured into Gary's yard again.

Gary took two weeks off from his firefighting job in late November 1997 to guide for Wapiti Basin Outfitters. A proud Montanan, he loved to show nonresident sportsmen the beauty and wildlife of the Big Sky State.

If you were a lazy hunter, Gary wasn't the guide for you. On the morning of November 25, Gary walked into the camp cook tent in Porcupine Basin about ten miles north of Yellowstone and discovered that his new group of clients was slow in getting going. He told them he wasn't going to baby any of them and that the success or failure of the hunt was up to them. If they couldn't get themselves together more quickly, they would lose the first hour of daylight, which is prime time for elk hunting.

As Gary turned to leave, one of the men asked if any bears were still out. Gary replied, "With a foot and a half of snow on the ground, the grizzlies should be in hibernation this late in the year, but with this warm wind blowing, I'd keep an eye open."

That made sense to Jay Wrobliske, a K-9 trainer for the narcotics division of the Houston Police Department in Texas. He liked Gary's style and hurried to get out of the tent to join him.

With Gary in the lead and Jay close behind, the men started working slowly through pockets of dense timber at the head of

Porcupine Basin where the elk liked to bed for the day. The warm weather had made the snow wet and sloppy, and both men struggled to keep their footing on the steep ground while maintaining a reasonably quiet pace.

At the brow of a small ridge, Gary approached a stand of tall lodgepole pines, with smaller pines flourishing below. A branch snapped in the pine thicket, followed by a thud. Both men tensed, straining their eyes, hoping to spot elk with antlers.

Without warning, a large sow grizzly burst from the thicket with a cub close behind. Jay snapped the rifle to his shoulder as the sow bore down on him, but the bear stopped fifteen feet away, popping her teeth and woofing. The sow, agitated to hysterics, spun round and round in a tight circle, stopping occasionally to pop her teeth again and bounce stiff-legged.

"Don't shoot her, Jay!" Gary ordered. "It's a bluff charge."

The sow scampered back ten yards to her cub, and that's when Gary reached for his bear spray. That movement caught the bear's attention, and she came at Gary in a low crouch, ears laid back and teeth showing. *This time,* Gary thought, *she means business.*

Without time to pull the can from its holster, Gary sprayed the sow from the hip when she was only ten feet away. Most of the spray missed, but it startled the bear, and she hesitated, then came at him again. This time he hit her with a good blast of bear spray at five feet as she was gathering herself for a final leap at him.

The sow instantly turned away, spinning in a tight circle. Then she galloped off with her cub. Both men sagged to the snowy, trampled ground. "Whew! That was close," Jay croaked when he finally found his voice. "I was a split second away from shooting her."

Gary nodded. "And then we'd have been in real trouble."

Gary credits the fortunate ending of the incident to the cool head kept by his client. "Jay's police job puts him in contact with lots of potentially dangerous people—some who bluff and some who mean business. That's the only thing that saved the bear, and maybe even us, from injury."

But Jay gives all the credit to his guide. "You could tell Gary cares a lot about bears, and he didn't want to kill that sow if at all possible. If Gary hadn't been so knowledgeable in bear behavior and pepper spray use, this whole thing could have had a much more serious outcome."

■ ■ ■

There is a common misconception among the public that the average hunter, hunting guide, or outfitter hates grizzlies and would prefer to shoot them on sight. About a dozen grizzlies are found shot every year in the Yellowstone and Glacier ecosystems, but this is usually the work of the rare slob hunter or trigger-happy outlaw who spends most of his time swilling beer and shooting roadside signs. Most hunters like the idea of sharing the woods with an animal as powerful and unyielding as the great bear.

Cody, Wyoming, resident Nate Vance, who outfitted for nineteen years in the vast Thoroughfare Wilderness just southeast of Yellowstone National Park, is vocal in his admiration and appreciation for the great bear. His camp is way, way back there, almost forty-six miles on horseback from the trailhead. It's remote, it's wild, and it's prime grizzly country. Nate likes this, even if it almost got him killed.

His appointment with fate began in the early-morning darkness when he crawled out of his cot in a tent next to the cook tent at his camp. He hoped to have the tent warmed and the stove hot when the cook came in to prepare breakfast for the half-dozen elk archery hunters in camp. As Nate stumbled into the cook tent, he heard a noise out back. Thinking the cook was out there gathering firewood, he hurried to help.

He took two steps beyond the back of the tent, saw no lantern, and knew that it couldn't be the cook. The thought, *It must be a bear* flashed through his mind. He sensed a presence in the darkness and turned to face it. An instant later his head exploded in a shower of stars.

When he regained consciousness, he was lying on the table in the cook tent. The grizzly had landed a tremendous blow to the side of his face, slicing a deep gash above his right eye and knocking him out. "I was very fortunate the bear knocked me out," Nate said. "Because I just laid there, the grizzly ignored me. If I would have moved, or run, or fought back, it probably would have worked me over pretty good."

Luckily one of the bowhunting clients was a surgeon. Without an anesthetic, Nate lay on the table while the doctor stitched him up. Nate had also received a concussion and was woozy for a few days, but he recovered quickly.

Two days later, a client bow-killed a large six-point bull elk late in the evening, so guide and hunter field-dressed the carcass and returned to camp before dark. The next morning the exuberant men returned to the kill, and the guide was in the process of removing the meat from the carcass when the hunter suddenly yelled "Bear!"

The guide whirled around and pulled out his .44 magnum

pistol. Sixty yards away a large sow grizzly with two cubs was coming at him fast. The guide shot the sow as she bore down on him, but the sow never slowed as she barreled into him. The bear had the guide's head in her mouth and was about to bite down when the man reached up and shot her twice more in the head area. The client, who also carried a pistol, ran up and shot the bear in the chest. The sow broke off the attack and ran away. Nate and a Wyoming wildlife official followed the blood trail for a half mile but lost it in a rainstorm. The sow's body was never found.

On the way back to camp, Nate's emotions were in turmoil. He had an injured guide and a grizzly that was either dead or wounded and very dangerous. Something else also terrified him. With the guide and client shooting wildly from all angles, the potential for an accidental shooting was great. He couldn't live with that.

Nate also realized they were fortunate to have avoided a tragedy. In two days, two people in his camp had been attacked by grizzlies and had escaped without serious injury. He didn't feel like his outfit was properly prepared, and after this trip was over, he set about making sure every employee and client would be safe from a future bear attack.

But Nate remained adamant about one thing. There weren't going to be a bunch of bear guns toted around. That, he felt, gave the wrong impression of sportsmen. "Here we are, telling people we like the grizzly," Nate said. "Yet we're armed to the teeth with guns hanging everywhere."

Nate attended a seminar in Cody given by Mark Matheny of UDAP Pepper Power, who explained how bear spray worked. Nate was impressed and furnished every guide with a can of bear pepper spray, and he sent letters to clients suggesting they also carry it.

It didn't take Nate Vance long to find a use for his bear spray. A grizzly came into camp one night, determined to get at the food stored in bear-proof containers. The horses were going berserk as the bear brazenly tore up the camp. Something had to be done quickly. Nate shot bullets above the bear's head, but it didn't faze it. Then he kicked up dirt at the bear's feet with several shots from his pistol, but the bear was not alarmed.

Nate found himself thirty feet from a large grizzly that showed no fear. It was the perfect time to find out how well bear pepper spray worked. He sent a blast of orange spray into the bear's face. The grizzly jerked backward, then bounded into the night and never returned to the camp.

But it was another incident that fully convinced Nate of the effectiveness of bear spray. A client he was guiding had just shot a bull elk, and Nate set about field-dressing the animal as dusk set in. He heard branches snapping in the dark forest above him, then heard the unmistakable, unnerving sound of massive jaws popping. Nate knew what would come next.

He dropped his knife and pulled out his bear spray a second before the big grizzly burst from the dense timber and charged with ears laid back. When the bear was twenty feet away, Nate sent a two-second blast into the bear's face. "I've never seen an animal charge so fast," he said, "then turn around and go the other way so fast."

Nate also believes a blast of bear pepper spray is great aversive conditioning for grizzly bears. "They're intelligent animals. If a human shoots a bear with pepper spray, it'll remember it the next time it encounters a human."

But Nate Vance also has a word of caution for those who put too much confidence in bear spray. "I don't think anyone who's ever been charged by a grizzly bear would have a false sense of security, whether they're carrying a gun or pepper spray. They come so fast, and they're so big. It's best not to get into those situations if at all possible because you never know what could happen."

■ ■ ■

While it's usually the guide who looks out for the client, there are times when the tables are turned. Guide Pat Poppe is only too glad to admit that he learned a valuable lesson on that day in 1997 when he led client Jim Farmer and helper Kim Cannon into the high country to hunt for bighorn sheep above Hidden Basin south of Cody, Wyoming.

Hidden Basin is well-known as prime bear habitat, so Pat kept a keen eye out for bear sign on the ride in. As they entered the barren, tundralike alpine country just below massive cliffs where the sheep lived, Pat felt confident that the bears were all well below them.

The men tied their horses to some stunted trees and then climbed above timberline. They eased out to a grassy ridge so Kim Cannon could set up his powerful spotting scope and glass the rocks across the canyon for sheep. Kim was in the lead when he jerked his head up and exclaimed, "Oh no! Here she comes!" Pat looked up and spotted a huge sow grizzly with three small cubs galloping toward them from eighty yards away.

Jim Farmer's rifle was stowed in the scabbard on his horse almost a hundred yards away. Pat's immediate thought was, *We have nothing to defend ourselves with. We're at the mercy of this bear.*

Kim jumped behind a tree on the left, while Pat dove behind a small tree beside him. When Pat looked up, he knew he was in big trouble. The sow had singled him out and was bearing down on him. Unknown to Pat, both Kim Cannon and Jim Farmer were carrying bear pepper spray.

Kim stood up and fumbled with a small black holster on his hip, finally unsnapping the top flap. Pat watched in bewilderment as Kim, unnerved by the bear's charge, pulled his Leatherman pliers out of the holster. In the excitement, he had gone for the wrong holster: his pepper spray was holstered on the other side. Pat thought Kim had lost his mind.

The bear was now only twenty yards away, rushing forward like a runaway train. Jim Farmer stepped forward, fumbled with the safety on his own can of bear spray, and finally pressed the trigger. But in his haste, he turned the nozzle backward and ended up spraying his own arm.

The spray's loud hiss caused the sow to skid to a halt and glance back at her cubs for a few seconds to make sure they were safe. The sow turned again, spotted Jim Farmer, and came at him in a furious rush, low to the ground with ears laid back. Jim pointed the can in the right direction and sprayed the bear at fifteen feet. By then, Kim Cannon also had his can of bear spray out and added more punch to Jim's cloud of spray. As the dense orange mist engulfed the sow's face, she swapped ends and ran back to her cubs, madly shaking her head and pawing at her face before disappearing over the ridge.

Pat said to me, "Until Jim Farmer pulled out that can, I wasn't even aware anything like pepper spray existed." He added, with a laugh, "I guess I live a sheltered life."

After seeing the effect the spray had on the bear, Pat began carrying it everywhere. Well, almost everywhere. Whenever he returned to the main camp, he usually hung it on a nail in his sleeping tent. It was a habit that he came to regret.

A group of clients and guides were enjoying a midafternoon meal in the main camp's cook tent when a hunter who had killed a bighorn ram two days before sauntered outside to admire his trophy, which was stored in a grove of trees next to a nearby creek. The sheep's horns were missing. Since everyone was joking and having a good time, the man guessed that a trick had been played on him. He ducked back into the cook tent and asked, "Okay, who's the wise guy who hid my sheep horns?"

It took several minutes and some earnest protest to convince the man that no one had hidden the horns. Everyone went outside to search for the missing trophy. Pat grabbed the camp's bear gun, a shotgun loaded with buckshot and slugs.

They followed a drag trail down to the creek, still unsure who, or what, had taken the prized horns. Suddenly a large silver-tipped boar grizzly burst out of the willows across the creek and charged the men. Pat snapped the shotgun to his shoulder and sent three lethal charges into the bear, then put a slug in its brain as it lay in the creek.

The horns were retrieved, but the killing left Pat with a bitter memory. "I like grizzlies. I really do. I just hated to kill that bear. If I'd kept my pepper spray on my hip while in camp, that bear would be alive today."

Only later did Pat learn that he may have done the wildlife community a favor. Like so many bears that suddenly show up in an area and cause problems, the 375-pound boar that Pat shot had a history. It had been live-trapped in Montana after killing domestic sheep and had been dropped off in a remote section of the Gallatin

Canyon north of Yellowstone. The bear had traveled more than a hundred miles south into Wyoming.

Pat said that tracks left in the snow by the boar made it obvious the bear had raided camps before. The grizzly had circled the camp, nosing forward, as if casing the place, before sneaking in to pilfer the sheep horns and some stored meat.

Another chilling side to this episode came when Pat followed the bear's tracks backward and discovered where the animal had followed the tracks of a client and guide who had left camp a few hours earlier. The bear had followed the men for a distance before turning back toward camp. Still fresh in Pat's mind was the fate of two British Columbia hunters who had shot a bull elk and were attacked and killed by a grizzly while field-dressing the carcass. That bear, it was believed, had been alerted and attracted to the opportunity arising from the hunters' shots.

Because of the nature of their work—slipping silently through the forest or gutting out an elk in the dark—hunting guides remain at greater risk of encountering a charging grizzly. Legally, they can kill it. Yet it is good to know that the majority of these hardy woodsmen harbor an admiration for the grizzly. As long as the great bear is not biting them or their clients, most guides prefer to live and let live.

CHAPTER 8

Bowhunters and Bears

Archery hunters shun the long-range capability of the high-powered rifle and purposely choose to hunt with an ancient weapon whose effective range is forty yards or less. Camouflaged from head to toe to hide their presence, they move silently through the deep woods, hoping to slip within forty yards of an elk or deer without being detected. Such purists cite the challenge of the close-range encounter, and not the kill, as the driving force behind their passion.

In grizzly country, the demands of this challenging sport can be a blueprint for disaster. The reasons are painfully clear. While knowledgeable hikers make lots of noise to alert a bear to their presence, bowhunters slip silently through the forest, wearing charcoal-impregnated clothing to mask their odor after having doused themselves with scent eradicator. And while recreationists hike only in daylight, keeping a keen eye out for fresh bear activity, bowhunters pad through the dark forest for miles to get to their favorite elk-hunting spot before daylight.

At some point, such activity leaves the realm of sport and becomes a requiem for the bowhunter. And if that isn't bad enough, there is another factor thrown into this equation: every fall a small army of archery hunters migrates to the western states to pursue the bull elk during the rut with little or no knowledge of the do's and don'ts of bear country. This headlong pursuit of the bull elk, while ignoring proper behavior in grizzly country, puts both hunter and bear at risk. With the rapid increase in grizzly numbers in the western states, and the corresponding expansion of grizzly range into areas long devoid of bears, the result has been a sharp increase in conflicts between grizzlies and bowhunters.

■ ■ ■

Michigan resident Russ Leach was ecstatic when his uncle, Rex Rogers of Colstrip, Montana, agreed to take him elk hunting into the Taylor Fork, a remote, pristine drainage in the lower Gallatin Canyon north of Yellowstone National Park. It had been Russ's dream to hunt the mighty bull elk with bow and arrow, but he could never accumulate enough money to afford a guided hunt. His uncle's invitation was a godsend.

When Russ arrived at Rex's home in Colstrip, his uncle asked him if he knew about bear spray. Russ replied that he had a pistol for self-defense, but his uncle knew this wasn't good enough. Though Rex had not seen a grizzly in thirteen years of bowhunting in the Taylor Fork, the presence of the bears was well documented. Rex told Russ that he'd feel a lot better if Russ purchased some bear pepper spray.

Russ agreed, but at the sporting goods store he balked. A can of bear spray and holster cost forty dollars. Russ said later that if his uncle had not been so insistent, he probably would not have purchased the spray. And this story might have had a far different ending.

On the first day of their hunt, Rex and Russ hiked about three miles into the Taylor Fork and set up camp. Russ was so excited he couldn't sleep that first night. At dawn he realized he was not ready to proceed with his plan to strike out on his own for his archery hunt. The high altitude had robbed his lungs of oxygen, and the sheer enormity of the wilderness was intimidating. He spent the first two days hunting near camp to acclimate himself to this strange new land.

On the morning of the third day, Russ set out on his own. He hiked about a mile before he heard his first bull elk bugle. It was a wild, primal sound—starting low, but increasing in volume and intensity until its hollow, screaming challenge echoed among the craggy peaks like the cry of a wilderness ghost.

Russ encountered several elk that morning but couldn't get a shot. Finally, the animals retreated into the dense timber thickets to bed down for the day. He curled up under a spruce tree and slept for hours as the warm, Indian summer sun drenched the land.

Russ awoke at 4:30 in the afternoon and munched some trail mix. The earlier encounters with elk had bolstered his enthusiasm and confidence, and he started out at 5:30 to find some more of the animals. He climbed onto a low ridge, where he blew into a commercially made elk bugle; immediately, two bulls bugled back from a series of openings a half mile away.

Russ slipped forward, searching for the bulls. He eased up to a meadow and peeked into it, but a small knoll in the middle obscured his vision. While studying the knoll, he spotted a patch of tan fur on its far side.

He was sure it was one of the bulls. Crouching low, he stalked toward the knoll. With breathless anticipation, he slipped forward to the crest. *Just a few more steps,* he thought, *and I'll have my first elk.*

Full of excitement, arrow nocked in the bowstring, he rose up to claim his prize. He immediately spotted two small bear cubs feeding about thirty yards away. His initial thought was, *What are two cubs doing here without . . . ?* Then he caught sight of the big, blond sow grizzly feeding forty yards away.

"The hair stood up on the back of my neck and I crouched down, thinking I could hide there until the bears fed away from me," Russ told me. "My plan worked until the sow fed around to the spot where I'd entered the opening. As soon as she cut my track, she whirled around and stood on her hind legs sixty yards away.

"She spotted me and didn't hesitate a second. She came at me like a freight train, low to the ground, with her ears laid back and teeth showing. I couldn't believe how fast she was moving.

"I pulled out my pistol with one hand, and my pepper spray with the other hand. Which should I use? I glanced up at the sow. She was twenty yards away and moving so fast that I doubted I could hit her with my pistol. But even as I raised the can of pepper spray, I wondered if the stuff would even work."

By then the charging grizzly was barely twenty feet away and barreling at him. Fighting the impulse to turn and run, Russ sent an orange cloud of bear spray into her face. The instant the spray hit the bear's nose, she wheeled and ran back to her cubs, then galloped into the timber. Heavy brush snapped and popped in the forest, and Russ heard the sow wheezing and rasping.

With the forest now quiet, Russ sank to his knees, and it was then that the enormity of what had just occurred hit him: he'd come within a fraction of a second of being torn apart by an enraged grizzly bear. Trembling spread throughout his body as he relived the frantic events. He'd had enough excitement for one day and started back to camp.

He hurried along a trail for twenty minutes, but the terrain became unfamiliar as the sun dipped low over the horizon. In his haste to get to the two bugling bulls, he hadn't paid enough attention to the route. Now he was unsure if the path he was following led back to camp—or to an angry sow grizzly looking for a rematch.

As dusk descended upon the forest, shadows lengthened and landmarks disappeared. Russ hurried in the direction he thought camp should be, using the beam of his flashlight to keep him on the trail—until the flashlight's beam dimmed and then flickered out. Russ pushed on for the next half hour, frantic to get back to camp before total blackness enveloped the deep forest. The thought of running into another grizzly in the night crossed his mind about a thousand times. Finally, he broke onto an open ridge and spotted the welcome glow of a lantern in a tent far below.

That night Russ recounted his ordeal to his uncle. Rex didn't need to remind Russ that the forty dollars he'd spent for pepper spray was money well spent. With grizzlies in the area, the men decided it would be best to hunt together.

Two days later, Russ and Rex were hunting a high subalpine area of open meadows separated by dense pockets of timber. Two bulls started bugling about three hundred yards ahead, and the men slipped forward to get within bow range. They eased to the edge of a meadow and spotted a huge six-point bull elk guarding his harem of fourteen cows. Russ moved sixty yards to the left and prepared for a shot. Three times the big bull passed by as he patrolled his harem, but he never presented a good shot. The bull suddenly became alert, then trotted into the forest with the cows following close behind.

Rex sneaked over to Russ and whispered, "What happened? Did the bull see you?"

Russ vigorously shook his head. "No, and the wind was in my face the whole time."

At a loss to explain the elk herd's sudden departure, the men advanced to the edge of the opening and immediately spotted the reason. A large, brown sow grizzly with three cubs had moved into the lower end of the meadow. Rex and Russ yelled and waved their arms to alert the sow to their presence. The sow stood up, spotted them, and ran away.

Two days later, after a hard evening hunt, the men decided they would sleep in and rest sore muscles. During breakfast at midmorning, Russ looked up and spotted a large black bear feeding on huckleberries high above camp. The black-bear hunting season had just opened, so Rex and Russ decided to make a long, downwind stalk on the bear and then approach it from above.

After an hour of hiking, they eased forward to a ridge top, expecting the black bear to be right below them and in bow range. But when they peeked over the ridge, they realized they'd made a serious mistake. The bear feeding thirty yards away was dark in color, but it wasn't a black bear. A huge, charcoal-colored boar grizzly grunted and chomped on low-bush huckleberries.

Rex stood up and yelled to alert the boar that they were in the area. The men were surprised when the big boar simply eyed them for a few seconds, then went back to stripping berries from the bushes.

Russ and Rex both bow-killed bull elk on that hunting trip, and they had no bear problems while packing out the meat. But they continued seeing bears. By the time they left, they had spotted thirteen grizzlies in the Taylor Fork drainage.

Russ summed up his first visit to grizzly territory: "I'd read a little about grizzlies, but I really didn't know much about them before my trip. After that sow charged me, I became a lot more careful about barging ahead in bear country.

"Once you have bears on your mind, it changes the way you walk and the way you think in bear country."

■ ■ ■

In contrast to the neophyte who stumbles into the jaws of disaster and miraculously escapes, there is the man whose attention to detail and dogged preparation give him the ability to function properly at a moment's notice.

Eric Burge has spent much of his life on the edge. He's a world traveler who has worked as a professional kayaker, filmed sharks off the coast of New Guinea, and served as a stunt coordinator in Hollywood. For Eric, life was a series of adrenaline rushes to be taken to the brink of disaster and then laughed at—until the day his best friend, an expert kayaker, drowned in front of his eyes.

The death changed Eric. He no longer flung himself into everything with reckless abandon. Oh, he maintained his devil-may-care lifestyle, but it became tempered with a determination to make sure that death was not the eventual winner. And that took preparation.

In memory of his friend, he became an expert in whitewater

safety and rescue, and he formed the habit of preparing for the unseen by visualizing problems and then mentally solving them. It was only natural, then, that Eric would look upon the possibility of a grizzly bear encounter with a more serious attitude than the average bowhunter.

For Eric to even partake in the hunt was a mild surprise to Eric's many friends. His mellow personality might give one the impression that he opposed the killing of animals. But Eric believes in the cycle of nature, where all things are used for the good of all: plants are grown and consumed by animals, and animals are used for sustenance. And as for natural food, Eric considered a sleek elk to be the epitome of natural food—high protein, low fat, and grown fresh and chemical-free in the wild.

But if he was to eat an elk, he decided, he would have to hunt for one. And if he was to kill to eat, it would be a personal experience not taken lightly. He would be responsible for the ebb of a wild animal's life in the most personal way he knew—a sharp arrow shot by a bow at close range. He practiced religiously until he hit a target consistently with his arrows. The killing would be more than a sport, more than a trophy; it would be the taking of life for the ultimate sacrifice—to transfer it to another.

Eric lives in Bozeman, Montana, and he planned to hunt in the game-rich Gallatin Canyon north of Yellowstone. Besides the cornucopia of vast elk herds, the Gallatin harbors another species in abundance—the grizzly bear. Eric considered a pistol for self-defense but decided against it, choosing bear pepper spray instead. But he didn't walk into a sporting goods store and purchase the first can pushed into his hands. He read extensively about pepper-based sprays, studied research documents about the sprays, and eventually chose UDAP Pepper Power.

He also studied grizzly bear behavior, pondered the essentials of self-defense in the rare event of a bear attack, then formulated a plan. Eric began visualizing a confrontation with a grizzly long before his fall bowhunt.

On the morning of October 6, 1998, Eric Burge parked at the trailhead to Tom Miner Basin. His plan was to hike into the high country in the Spanish Peaks Wilderness and live out of a camp while he pursued bull elk.

For three miles, he trudged steadily uphill while carrying a heavy backpack and bow. The midmorning sun was burning the frost away as Eric moved briskly along the Middle Creek Trail. Just ahead, the forest ended and the treeless alpine landscape began. Eric spotted a low area between hills close by and decided this saddle would be a perfect place to set up camp. He put on an extra spurt, anxious to get there and remove the heavy pack from his aching shoulders.

Forty yards from the saddle, he heard a noise and glanced up to see a brown hump coming over the crest. He froze as a large, brown sow grizzly and two almost-grown cubs ambled into sight and started down the trail toward him.

Eric stepped off the trail and switched the bow from his right hand to his left, then drew the pepper spray from its hip holster. That movement alerted the sow, who jerked her head up at forty yards, her eyes wide with surprise. The next instant she was in a full charge, head down, ears laid back. *This stuff better work,* Eric thought as he raised the can of bear spray.

When the sow was thirty feet away, Eric shot a short burst of spray, but a stiff crosswind caught most of it and sent it to the side.

Still, enough residue hung in the air to make the sow hesitate. Then she ran around the drifting orange cloud and came at Eric again. At twelve feet, he gave her another burst, this time hitting her in the face. The sow stopped, pawed at the ground, flailed at the air, but stumbled forward a few more steps. At eight feet, he blasted her again in the face. The sow stopped and madly pawed at the air, spun around twice, then galloped down the trail with the two confused cubs trailing behind.

"It was so surreal," Eric said later. "One minute I'm walking up this incredibly beautiful mountainside, and the next instant I'm in the middle of this life-and-death struggle with an enraged sow grizzly right in front of me. Then it's all quiet again.

"It made me wonder for a few seconds if I had just imagined the whole thing. But then I looked down at the half-empty can of pepper spray in my right hand, and my eyes smarted a little from the spray in the air. When I looked down and saw the bear tracks in the trail, I knew it was no muse."

Forgotten now was any thought of hunting elk. Eric just wanted out of there, but he had a serious problem. The sow had run down the trail he'd just hiked up. No way was he going to hike back down that path. He hurried to the top of the ridge and made a mile-wide circle around the Middle Creek drainage. He stayed in the open as much as possible to avoid another confrontation with a bear because his can of bear spray was almost empty.

There were times during his trek when he was forced to enter dense forest. As Eric entered a particularly gloomy draw choked with deadfall and dense brush, he thought, *This is the kind of place a grizzly would choose for a day bed.* Seconds later the forest erupted fifty yards to his right, and Eric spun around, bear spray in hand, ready to meet the charge. A herd of elk galloped away.

Emotionally spent, Eric hurried down the heavily forested mountainside, but on a ridge covered with whitebark pine, whose seeds are a favorite bear food, he made an unsettling discovery. Beside a tree trunk he found a pair of 7-by-30 Leupold binoculars lying on the ground—moss-covered, the leather straps rotted away.

After his tumultuous day, the find was disturbing. Who would leave an expensive pair of binoculars in the middle of nowhere? His eyes swept the forest floor for bones, but he was anxious to get out of that country as fast as possible, and he quickly left. Looking back on the incident, Eric wonders if those dark woods don't hide another, more tragic bear story than his.

Eric said of his grizzly attack, "People think they'll have time when a bear attacks, but mine happened so fast I didn't have time to think things out. I just had time to react. From the time the sow spotted me to the time I sprayed was no more than three seconds. That's why I chose a hip holster and a pepper spray that could be shot from the hip.

"It also occurred to me that most of the bear attacks I'd read about happened in seconds, so I got into the habit of looking ahead at a rock and imagining a bear suddenly jumping out from it and me spraying it. I did it over and over again in my mind so I wouldn't have to use any logical thought process to function."

Eric summed up the attack: "I was just amazed how fast a 400-pound grizzly could move. And the rage in those eyes! That I'll never forget."

■ ■ ■

Besides the obvious hazards of bowhunting in grizzly country, Wyoming resident David Nyreen carried another burden whenever he entered the woods. It seemed that wherever David went, a bear encounter was not far off. It got to the point where his friends, with knowing winks, began calling him Bear Magnet.

Like the time he and his dad were sleeping in the camper shell of his pickup: in the middle of the night, David awoke and felt the camper rocking. Each man thought the other was playing a joke, but they froze as loud grunts emanated from the cab of the pickup. When David peeked out, he spotted a young grizzly bear working furiously to break through the side window and get at the food stored inside. Loud yelling and pounding scared the bear away, but a series of bear incidents that followed made David wonder if there wasn't some truth to the Bear Magnet moniker his friends had laid upon him.

A terrifying incident the next year cemented David's dubious distinction as a bear magnet. He was gun-hunting with two friends when they killed an elk four miles from the trailhead. They hustled to field-dress the carcass and get it out of the backcountry before the meat spoiled in the warm weather.

Darkness overtook them as they struggled along the trail, burdened by heavy packs loaded down with elk meat. As they trudged along the moonlit path, all three men began to feel uneasy. David was in the rear, and for no discernible reason the hair on the back of his neck began to stand up. Then he heard a branch snap in the dark timber behind him. *Maybe it's just a deer,* he thought, but he knew better.

The lead man suddenly halted and whispered, "Listen." Off to the side, a deep guttural grunt floated back through the night air, followed by the popping of teeth. The men squinted into the darkness and saw the dark form of a bear moving through the moonlight forty yards away.

The men yelled, and the bear responded by popping its teeth and growling even louder. Then there was silence, and along with it came the hope that the bear had moved off. But when they began hiking again, they heard the bear moving nearby, first behind them, then on their right side. The moon disappeared behind the clouds, and it became a terrifying hike, not knowing where, when, or if the bear would suddenly charge out of the night. The ordeal continued for three miles until they approached the trailhead where the pickup was parked. Only then did the bear melt away into the dark of the night.

David got serious about finding something that would keep him safe in bear country. He considered a .44 magnum pistol, but he didn't want to pack the extra weight. And like so many sportsmen, he felt a grudging admiration for the great bear and didn't want to shoot a grizzly. But neither did he want to be killed by one. After researching bear pepper sprays, he bought a can of it to carry in a holster at his side.

As the fall of 1996 approached, David Nyreen looked upon the upcoming elk archery season with optimism. He'd taken more than a dozen backcountry hiking and fishing trips into prime grizzly habitat that summer without a single bear incident. Maybe he'd finally shed the curse of being a bear magnet.

On August 31, David, his uncle Harold Kaiser, and his friend Jim Dunkerly started in on horseback for Torrent Creek, a steep, heavily timbered drainage in northwestern Wyoming a few miles south of Yellowstone National Park. Opening day of elk archery season began the next day, plus Harold had also drawn a coveted bighorn sheep tag. They had penetrated fifteen miles into the wilderness and were encouraged by the lack of bear sign. Jim Dunkerly's horse threw a shoe, so he decided to turn back and have his horse tended to, with the promise that he'd be back sometime the next day.

After establishing camp, David and Harold hiked above the camp and soon spotted several bighorn rams in the rocks farther up. Two large bull elk and several cows fed in an alpine meadow below. The men decided to go after the elk in the morning with their bows.

They started up a ridge about an hour before daylight, but it was too open, so they dropped into a creek bottom where they could advance out of sight of the elk. At first the going was easy and they made good time, but as the canyon narrowed, they struggled over logjams and several times had to wade the stream. Tired and wet, they decided to climb out of the creek bottom to the ridge high above.

By the time they staggered to the crest, it was too late in the morning to go after the elk, so David and Harold sat down in the shade of a grove of trees to rest and eat a sandwich. Suddenly they heard a loud crashing in the trees fifty yards away. With visions of a trophy bull elk bursting into the open, both men scrambled for cover.

David was well hidden behind a large red fir tree, ready to draw back his bow when the big bull stepped into range, but his uncle yelled three words that sent a chill up his spine: "Here she comes!"

David peeked out and sucked in a quick breath as a sow grizzly thundered past, with her two confused cubs hanging back. For a moment, it appeared the bear would continue on her way, but she turned at forty yards and began circling in an agitated, stiff-legged gait while gnashing her teeth. The sow suddenly jerked upright when she again caught the men's scent and she ran toward them, though she still hadn't seen them.

"So far, the sow had her ears up, and she was bouncing stiff-legged," David told me. "I could see she was upset, but not in an attack mode. Then our eyes met, and she immediately laid her ears back and rushed at me. I knew she wasn't going to stop."

David grabbed the pepper spray from his hip holster and sprayed the oncoming grizzly at twenty feet, but he didn't hit her with a full blast. Still, it stopped the bear's charge. She circled around the tree to the right, massive jaws snapping in David's face, while she maneuvered for a clear charge. The sow lunged forward again, and this time David blasted her full in the face at ten feet.

The sow jerked backward and ran uphill to her cubs, coughing and madly shaking her head, before bounding into the timber over the ridge.

"I wasn't too scared during the attack," David said, "but after it was over, my legs started shaking so badly I could hardly stand up. Uncle Harold wasn't much better. I'd used up most of the nine-ounce can of spray during the attack, so we didn't want to stay around there just in case the sow came back. We slowly backed away, then hurried back to camp."

David shakes his head and chuckles about one aspect of the incident. "There were two of us in front of that grizzly, and my uncle was actually a bit ahead of me. Naturally, the sow ran past him and came after me.

"When I got back to town I went out and bought the bigger fifteen-ounce can of pepper spray. When you're a bear magnet, you need all the help you can get."

CHAPTER 9

Photographers and Bears

Wildlife photography is almost as dangerous as bowhunting in bear country. Some say it's even more dangerous. That's because stealth and an unobtrusive presence are as much a part of an outdoor shutterbug's outfit as a camera and telephoto lens. These laudable attributes allow a photographer to move unnoticed among wild animals. If that wild animal happens to be a furtive little deer, no problem. If it's a grizzly, big problem.

Wildlife photographer Tim Christie, whose photos appear in outdoor and nature books and magazines, found that out when he took a short walk to snap a few photos of deer and ended up almost dead. Tim was driving along Camas Road in Glacier National Park in October 1987, looking for any photo subject. A hundred yards ahead, two whitetail bucks trotted across the road and headed for a secluded meadow a short distance from the pavement.

Tim pulled his pickup off the road and wavered for a few seconds, trying to decide whether he should take the time to replace his light tennis shoes with sturdy hiking boots before going after the deer. Tim has weak ankles, and he almost never goes afield without boots. But these were big bucks, perfect magazine cover material, and they'd be gone soon. So he grabbed his camera gear and slipped into the dense forest in his tennis shoes with the thought, *It won't be too bad. I'll be close to the road.*

Tim shadowed the bucks as they fed along the edge of the meadow, staying back about a hundred yards to avoid pressuring the animals. Using his 600-millimeter lens, Tim shot several rolls of film as passing vehicles roared by just out of sight behind him.

Suddenly the bucks stiffened and stared nervously at a thicket of trees to his right. Tim wondered if another photographer was coming, or maybe a ranger was checking on him. The deer had been aware of his distant presence and had not shown alarm, so he was a bit perplexed when they bounded into the forest. But Tim was also a student of wildlife behavior, and he was well aware of the furtive nature of the white-tailed deer, so he merely shrugged and turned back, content with the photos he had taken.

He'd walked only a short distance with the camera and tripod slung over his shoulder when he caught sight of a small brown animal moving out of the thicket. A tiny cub stepped into the open, spotted him, and began squealing.

It's a grizzly, Tim thought. He immediately discarded his camera gear and looked for a tree to climb. A limby red fir stood just ten yards away, and he scrambled onto it. As he worked his way up through the limbs, Tim heard crashing through the brush, followed by growling. Then the tree shook so hard he almost fell out. He looked down into the eyes of a snarling sow grizzly just a few feet below. That gave him incentive to quickly climb higher.

Tim breathed a sigh of relief to be sitting fifteen feet above the bear, secure in the knowledge that grizzlies can't climb trees. The sow was not aware of that fact, because she started up the tree after him.

"She came up as fast as I had," Tim said. "She just hooked her paws over the branches and pulled herself up. I was frantic. I was almost to the top of the tree, and she was right behind me."

Tim climbed until the tree trunk became too thin. He glanced down, and the sow was right there, jaws snapping mere inches from his feet.

The tree limbs were spindly, but Tim frantically tried to climb a foot higher. He glanced down just as the sow launched upward and clamped her jaws onto the heel of his right tennis shoe. "It felt like my foot was in a vice," Tim said. "I really thought she'd snap my heel off."

The sow released her grip around the tree trunk and all 300 pounds of bear just hung there, pulling on Tim. His hands were slowly losing their grip around the tree as the bear continued to jerk and pull; the bear was about to pull him out of the tree and have her way with him on the ground.

Then Tim felt his tennis shoe slip off his foot and glanced down to see the bear, shoe still in its mouth, crashing down through the limbs. Not only was he fortunate that the shoe came off his foot, but the falling grizzly also wiped out most of the limbs, making another assault near impossible.

The sow, still agitated, loped over to a large blown-down spruce tree and climbed to the top of the root wad. "It was really unsettling," Tim said, "because when she stood on her hind legs, she was almost at my level."

Even during this traumatic moment in his life, the photographer in Tim Christie surfaced as he thought, *Gee, she has the most beautiful eyes. I wish I had a camera.* The sow punctuated that thought with a surly *woof!* and scampered away with her cub.

"I was less than a hundred yards from my car," Tim said, "but I didn't want to chance coming down, not knowing where the bear was. A couple times other vehicles stopped next to mine, and I yelled my lungs out to get their attention, but they drove off. After an hour I slowly shinnied down the tree and hurried to my car."

Tim's experience with the sow grizzly prompted him to do some hard thinking about his wildlife photography profession. He now takes fewer chances and has started carrying bear pepper spray. "I think it's insane," he says, "for anyone in bear habitat to take to the woods without it."

■ ■ ■

Conrad Rowe and Michael Francis, also professional wildlife photographers, agree wholeheartedly with Tim Christie. Fortunately it didn't take a near-death experience for both men to carry bear spray as a vital part of their camera gear. A wise choice, considering the predicament they found themselves in while photographing a bull elk near Jasper in Canada's Banff–Jasper National Park.

The two men had become good friends after meeting while photographing elk in Yellowstone. In 1996 they made plans to rendezvous at the Whistler Campground just outside Jasper and team up to photograph rutting bull elk. Both men carried Counter Assault bear spray.

On the frosty morning they got together, they were photographing a big bull elk that was rutting near an old road. Impatient to find some cows, the bull set out at a fast pace toward a meadow two hundred yards away. Michael and Conrad followed at a safe distance.

The bull entered the meadow and turned left. Conrad followed, staying back in the trees. As he edged forward, he spotted movement out of the corner of his eye and turned to find a large brown grizzly forty yards away, coming toward him.

"The first thing that entered my mind," Conrad said, "was to warn Michael. I yelled, 'Michael, a grizzly!' I left my camera and tripod and started backing away, looking for a tree to climb while Michael edged my way."

The bear, now twenty yards away, was coming fast. Michael waved his arms and yelled, and that caused the bear to veer to the right, thereby exposing two tiny cubs. "As soon as I saw the cubs," Conrad said, "I glanced over at Michael, and we both yelled, 'Get out your spray!'

"The sow ignored Michael and came at me low and fast. It was obvious she wasn't going to stop. We both sprayed her at about six feet. She got hit good with a heavy blast of spray, and it stopped her like she'd run into a wall. She spun around, bellowing, and ran back into the heavy timber with her cubs."

■ ■ ■

Tim Christie, Michael Francis, and Conrad Rowe are ethical photographers who care for the welfare of the animals they photograph. Sadly, there is another breed of photographer roaming the wilds whose blind ambition to secure coveted bear photographs has led to wanton disregard for the welfare of the bears.

Montana bear management specialist Tim Manley, during our interview, shook his head and complained, "In my opinion, wildlife photographers are some of the worst habituators of bears. It's a well-known fact that a habituated bear, having lost its fear of humans, is going to end up dead sooner or later unless it's rehabilitated. Yet I've seen photographers do the dumbest, most dangerous things in their headlong zeal to get the close-up shot."

Standing out in Manley's memory is a case that unfolded near Polebridge, Montana, a village on the banks of the North Fork Flathead River along Glacier National Park's western boundary. As reported in the *Missoulian* newspaper, residents began noticing an increase in bear activity in 1997. Grizzly sightings had averaged one or two per year. Now they were seeing more than a dozen a year, and the bears had begun to act strangely. In the past the bears ran away when confronted by a human, but now they walked brazenly through front yards and ignored barking dogs and yelling humans. Tim Manley was at a loss to explain the sudden increase in bear activity.

Later that year, Forest Service surveyors working in the area reported an unusually large number of grizzlies, and when Manley investigated, he quickly discovered the reason. Fifty-pound bags of corn, oats, and barley were strewn on the ground around the property of a wildlife photographer.

"There was bear scat all over the place, filled with corn, oats, and barley," Manley said. "The feed was so thick on the ground that it would require machinery to remove all of it."

The photographer claimed it was leftover grain from winter feeding of deer and elk to keep them from starving. After strongly advising the man that placing out any kind of feed would bring in bears, Manley used aversive conditioning methods such as shooting rubber bullets against their rumps to put the fear of humans back into the bears and drive them into the deep woods. Concerned that the scattered corn would bring in more bears, the state even strung an electric fence around the man's property.

The next winter, the photographer announced that he intended to feed the deer and elk again. Tim Manley visited him and strongly discouraged the practice. The man, known as a bear lover, compromised and said he would place the grain on his frozen pond. That way, he explained, by the time the bears came out of hibernation in spring the corn would have sunk to the bottom of the pond. Manley just shook his head at that odd reasoning.

The next spring, Manley was tracking a radio-collared female grizzly. The bear led him to the photographer's property—and to a pile of birdseed hidden behind a log. Manley discovered other piles of birdseed and grain behind logs and stumps.

When confronted, the man claimed the grain and seeds were for ducks. This time Manley didn't buy it. "He told me he wasn't going to feed the bears anymore," Manley said, "but I firmly believe he was putting the grain out in strategic places, hidden from sight, so he could photograph grizzlies." Unfortunately the state's hands were tied. It is illegal to feed bears in national parks, such as nearby Glacier, and on national forest land, but not on private property.

And then fate intervened. Manley was waiting in a Salt Lake City airport for a flight when he noticed a copy of *National Wildlife* magazine with an article about grizzly bears promoted on its cover. When he saw the photographer's name, his pulse rate shot up, and when he opened the magazine to the article, his blood ran hot. Real hot.

"The photograph showed a sow grizzly and cub climbing on a supposed abandoned bird feeder in the Flathead National Forest," Manley said. "I knew exactly where that bird feeder was located—about twenty feet behind the guy's house. I recognized other bears, too. They were problem bears I'd been dealing with."

Even when confronted with evidence that he'd been baiting grizzlies onto his property to photograph them for financial gain, the man continued to deny any wrongdoing. The state considered charging him with baiting and endangering bears, but the laws were so vague that officials reluctantly dropped the case.

Not Tim Manley. He wrote to the magazine and told the editor that the manner in which the photo was taken had created exactly the conditions the author complained other people were causing. Local newspapers ran stories detailing the incident, and the state of Montana began looking into the possibility of prohibiting bear-baiting practices even on private land.

"It's ironic that the cub in that magazine article about saving the grizzly is no longer alive," Manley said. "It was illegally killed, largely due to its habituation to people. It died with a belly full of birdseed."

The photographer later sold the property and moved on, leaving Manley with the herculean task of rehabilitating the bears. "There were about a dozen bears feeding on that property when the guy left," Manley said, "and they picked up bad habits that will cause problems with local residents for years. We've had to use Karelian bear dogs, rubber bullets, and other adverse conditioning methods to put the fear of man back in them."

Two years later Manley was still dealing with fallout from the situation. "Late last fall," Manley said, "we had a young sow grizzly walk right into the town of Whitefish and start eating apples under trees. We trapped and relocated her up north in the Whitefish Mountain Range. She hibernated there over the winter, but when she came out of her den in the spring, she headed north for thirty miles in a straight line and ended up on the property where the bait had been placed out, looking for corn and birdseed."

■ ■ ■

You'd think it couldn't get any worse than that, but it does. A report in June 1998 in the *Hungry Horse News,* of Columbia Falls, Montana, told of a group of hikers that had banded together on the trip from Red Rocks Lake to the trailhead in the Swiftcurrent Area on Glacier National Park's east side. Among the hikers was an amateur photographer hoping to get some bear photos.

When the group rounded a corner, they spotted a yearling grizzly bear above the trail. The curious young bear began following the hikers at a distance. Anxious to get some close grizzly pictures, the photographer advanced toward the bear— ignoring warnings from the group that what he was doing was illegal and dangerous.

The man wasn't overly concerned, since it was a smallish bear. And besides, he carried a pistol illegally brought into the park, concealed under his jacket. At first the bear retreated, but with the photographer pressuring it, the bear began walking stiff-legged and then turned to face its antagonist.

The photographer continued taking pictures of the agitated bear, holding the camera in one hand and the pistol in the other. Finally the bear had enough. It began popping its teeth and making bluff charges. Now frightened, the man fired warning shots above the bear's head and into the dirt. Then he backed away and hurried past the hikers.

If not for the quick thinking of a teenager in the group who had videotaped the incident, the man might have escaped punishment. The group alerted a ranger, and the man was cited for illegally carrying a weapon inside a national park.

I also witnessed the disregard some photographers show toward the welfare of bears. It was the spring of 1996, and I was taking pictures of black bears feeding along Camas Road in Glacier. Hoping to escape the crowds of people who cruised the road to view the bears, I turned onto a little-used side road. I came around a corner and spotted a medium-size black bear standing in the open, with a man photographing the bruin from about thirty yards away.

I grabbed my camera and tripod and eased out of my car to join the man. He looked back and frowned when he saw me. I assumed his look of dismay grew from his reluctance to share the photo opportunity. As I moved closer, he grabbed his gear and hurried away without a word. A minute later his car roared off.

The man's abrupt departure left me frowning, but the bear's actions had me even more perplexed. Rather than grazing on the new grass shoots, the bear seemed intent on pawing and chewing at something. And then I saw it—the flash of metal. *Could that guy have been feeding this bear?* I wondered.

After the bear wandered off, I walked over and found a well-chewed tuna fish can that reeked of bacon grease. The next day I found another chewed tuna can lying near a meadow where bears often appeared. My guess is that the guy had filled cans with the smelly bacon grease and was enticing wary bears to leave the safety of the dark forest and move into optimum camera position by throwing the grease-filled cans into sunny places with the best background. (Unfortunately I had failed to notice the license number on his car, which carried Washington state plates.)

■ ■ ■

Photographers who feed a bear for the purpose of luring the animal into close camera range usually escape prosecution and injury. But the habituated bear they leave behind is a danger to the next unsuspecting photographer who encounters it. Such was the case, as reported in the *Anchorage Daily News,* in what happened to Michio Hoshino, a wildlife photographer who lived in Anchorage, Alaska. In his native Japan, Michio often hosted wildlife programs on the nature channel.

In July 1997, Michio arrived on Kamchatka Island in Russia's remote chain of Far East islands. The place was famous for its large population of brown bears that showed up at the Khakeetsin River rapids to feed on spawning salmon. Michio was guiding a Japanese film crew that was gathering material for a TV program. He also planned to photograph bears on his own.

There was an immediate problem. The summer salmon run was late, resulting in only a few brown bears roaming the area near the rapids, waiting impatiently for the fish to arrive. Some of these bears went hungry; others took matters into their own hands. The week before, a big boar had broken out a window in the single lodging cabin on the island and climbed through it and ransacked the place. Newly arrived photographers quickly boarded up the window and moved into the cabin. But with several photographers and the Japanese crew inside with all their gear, there was not enough room for everyone, so Michio

Hoshino chose to sleep outside in a tent beside the crowded cabin.

Several nights while he slept in the tent, the big boar roamed through the camp, working feverishly but unsuccessfully to break into the underground food cache. A Russian photographer tried a number of times to use bear pepper spray on the bear, but the animal had learned to stay just far enough away to avoid the spray.

In the meantime, the photographers were growing as impatient as the bears. A cameraman from a Russian TV station arrived by helicopter and, finding the bears in short supply, did the wrong thing. Several times the man was observed feeding the big boar to get close shots. Not content with the paltry offerings of the Russian cameraman, the surly boar broke out the windows of the man's helicopter in its drive to get at the food stored inside.

Before this information could be spread to everyone in the camp, the salmon run began, putting aside any concern about the problem bear. With the salmon crowding through the rapids, even the big boar was seen fishing. Everyone thought the worst was over with this animal. They did not know that a habituated bear, hooked on human food rewards, is an incorrigible animal who has lost much of its natural fear of people and who maintains an insatiable desire for people's food even when natural food is abundant.

That night, the photographers in the cabin were startled awake by a man screaming outside. They heard Michio Hoshino yell over and over again, "Tent! Bear! Tent! Bear!" The men dashed outside, armed with a single can of bear spray, and saw Michio's tent being destroyed by the big boar.

They yelled and threw things at the bear, but the beast didn't even raise its head. One photographer grabbed a pail and shovel and banged loudly from just five yards away. The bear finally raised its head, eyed the man, then took Michio's limp body in its massive jaws and carried it into the darkness. The next day, a professional Russian hunter arrived and shot the boar from a helicopter. What was left of Michio Hoshino's body was then recovered. By that time, the Russian cameraman who had fed the boar was long gone—and no doubt receiving accolades for his ability to get so close to a bear.

■ ■ ■

Al Johnson paid a high price for his close-up photos of bears. Johnson, an Alaska state game biologist, had been sent to Denali National Park to photograph moose and other wildlife. Al was an experienced photographer, and on this trip he carried a 1,000-millimeter lens (which has about twenty-power magnification), along with 300- and 105-millimeter lenses for closer work.

While driving through the park, Al spotted a sow grizzly with three cubs about a half mile away. He brought along all three lenses as he hurried toward the bears. He didn't pressure the bears, staying back more than a hundred yards on the downwind side to avoid alarming the animals—and he always kept a good-size spruce tree close at hand, just in case.

As the story is told in Larry Kaniut's *Alaska Bear Tales,* Al followed the bears for more than two hours, using the 1,000-millimeter lens to capture crisp images as the bears fed on huckleberries in the brilliant autumn sun. But by late afternoon, the light was beginning to fade, making it difficult to use the light-hogging longer lens. The bears were also ambling closer to the road and away from the larger trees that Al sought for safety.

At this point, Al Johnson's desire for the perfect bear photo caused him to abandon the caution he'd so prudently employed throughout the afternoon, and he joined the cadre of wildlife photographers who have pushed their luck too far.

Al decided to lure the bears back toward his position with a predator call, a device that, when you blow into it, simulates the distress cry of a small animal. The call has been known to bring in a predator such as a bear, looking for an easy meal.

Al sought the largest spruce in the area, about eight inches in diameter at the base, and climbed to about fifteen feet. He began using the predator call, hoping the bears would come close to investigate and that he would then be able to use the shorter lenses.

At first there was no visible response from the bears. Then the cubs stood on their hind legs, but the sow still ignored the call. After five minutes of wailing on the call, Al was about to stick it back in his pocket and return to his vehicle when the sow began to show interest.

She looked in Al's direction for a few minutes, then headed toward the tree in a circular path. When the sow was forty yards away, Al yelled to stop her so he could begin taking photos, but his voice had no visible effect on the sow, though the cubs stopped and milled around about thirty yards from the tree. Al began taking pictures of the cubs as the sow continued toward the base of the tree.

Al heard the sow below, but the lower limbs obscured his vision. However, he heard her grunt and slap at his pack, which he had left at the base of the tree. The sow then continued past the tree and stood, waiting for the cubs.

Al was adjusting the focus on his camera when one of the cubs spotted him and began squealing. The sow instantly charged the tree, and a short time later Al felt a tremendous impact as the bear hit the trunk.

Because of the dense foliage, Al didn't know what was happening below, though he could hear branches snapping and claws scraping on the tree. As he squinted down through the limbs, he was horrified to see the sow's head and shoulders burst through the foliage. The bear's jaws clamped onto the heel of his hiking boot. An instant later, he was being dragged down through the branches.

As soon as he hit the ground, Al covered his face with his arms. The sow pounced, biting his arms. Then she gnawed at his skull, removing pieces of his scalp. Several times the sow was distracted by her cubs and stopped the attack long enough to look over and make sure they were safe. She returned each time to biting and pawing at Al.

Throughout the entire ordeal, Al played dead. After what seemed like an eternity to the ravaged man, the sow ran off in the direction of her cubs. As soon as the bear was out of sight, Al struggled to his feet and stumbled three hundred yards to his vehicle. A short time later a park employee who had been a registered nurse stopped and administered first aid. Another vehicle stopped, and Al was taken to park headquarters. He was rushed to a hospital, where he spent two weeks. He has since recovered.

■ ■ ■

Wildlife photography is one of the most coveted occupations among shutterbugs. And why not? You get paid to roam the great outdoors among a variety of wildlife. But there is a downside. The quality telephoto lenses required to get crisp close-up photos of reclusive wild animals from long distance can cost ten thousand dollars or more. An enthusiastic amateur, anxious to move up to professional status, can sometimes avoid this cost by using smaller lenses and getting closer to the animals. With benign animals such as deer and elk, it's doable. With a grizzly bear, it's a death wish.

Montana resident Bill Tesinsky was an amateur photographer who had found some success selling his wildlife photos. He had done admirably well with just an inexpensive camera and a 200-millimeter lens, which is considered too small to get the coveted close-ups that galleries and magazines seek and will pay well for. Bill had relied on his abilities as a woodsman to stalk in close, undetected by the animals.

Tesinsky had one big hole in his photography portfolio. He lacked grizzly bear photos. He knew the market was ripe for good grizzly shots, especially the close-ups that showed the beauty and power of the great bear.

In October 1987, Tesinsky drove to Yellowstone National Park to find a grizzly. He got lucky, in a manner of speaking, when he spotted a smallish female grizzly near the road a few miles south of the Canyon Village area. The bear was well-known to park rangers, having a remarkable ability to feed close to roads while accommodating the crowds of people who quickly jammed the pavement for a look at her. But she had also become a pest and had been trapped and relocated several times, each time quickly returning to her favorite haunts near Canyon Village.

No one saw or heard anything of Tesinsky for three days. Rangers finally investigated on foot. They quickly found the female grizzly, jealously guarding the remains of Bill Tesinsky. Because the bear had not only killed a human, but had also fed on the flesh, the rangers were ordered to kill the bear.

From evidence pieced together afterward, authorities speculate that Tesinsky followed the bear up a draw, no doubt easily coming close while the bear dug for roots and rodents. But Tesinsky encountered a problem that threatened to ruin this most fortunate encounter. The bear had a bright orange radio collar around her neck, which would render the photographs useless.

Unless, that is, he could somehow make the collar disappear. Most wildlife photographers know from experience that the large head of a grizzly, when looking directly at the camera, effectively hides the collar. Tesinsky probably knew this, so he apparently proceeded to use his stalking ability to get within the thirty-yard range needed to get effective photos with the little 200-millimeter lens.

Then something went very wrong. When she was feeding along the road, this grizzly had ignored up to a hundred humans clamoring around close by. But away from the road, the bear probably became alarmed and agitated by the sudden intrusion upon her safety zone. Exactly how the attack went down remains a mystery. What is known is that the bear had been feeding on the body for three days and had cached parts of it in holes.

The incident was given widespread exposure in the newspapers, and Tesinsky's fatal mistake of advancing toward the bear became the subject of many conversations among wildlife photographers. It was hoped that some good would come from Tesinsky's death, by serving to illustrate to others the danger of approaching a grizzly. Not everyone got the message.

Six months later, Montana resident Chuck Gibbs was hiking along the southern edge of Glacier National Park with his wife when he spotted a sow grizzly and three cubs. He sent his wife ahead to the trailhead. Gibbs, known as a great admirer of bears, felt that if he showed respect toward the animal, it would not hurt him. He was wrong.

When he didn't return, authorities were notified, and they soon discovered Gibbs's ravaged body lying among his photography equipment. Investigating rangers were surprised to find a .45-caliber pistol in Gibbs's backpack, unfired. When the film was developed, early frames showed a sow with two cubs at long range and appearing unconcerned, with succeeding frames showing the bears closer and closer, with the sow appearing more and more agitated. The last images show the sow looking his way from a distance of about fifty yards, then advancing toward the camera. The sow had not fed on the body, and the decision was made not to kill her because she had acted in defense of her cubs.

■ ■ ■

One solution to the problem of fledgling wildlife photographers putting themselves, and the bears, at risk would be for recognized professionals to step forward and speak out against taking chances. But sometimes these very professionals are the source of unwise behavior around bears.

A good example is provided in a story that appeared in the *Bozeman Daily Chronicle,* featuring the work of an internationally known wildlife photographer. In the article, the man said, "Most people think wildlife photographers are using 1,000 millimeter lenses. The closer the better, I say. You get better images. About 80 percent of my work is shot with an 80-200 millimeter lens."

The photographer proudly recounted a recent black-bear photo trip. "I was able to follow the bears on their daily routines. Three of the five of them were confident enough to let me tag along through the brush. I was charged many times. When a sow charged, I just stood my ground. They would hit the brush and try to intimidate me."

The man went on to say that he's more afraid of ticks and Lyme disease than of bears. But he just hasn't met the wrong bear yet. Bill Tesinsky did; so did Chuck Gibbs.

Wildlife photographers should follow the first commandment of proper behavior in bear country: never advance toward a bear. In our national parks, it is not only illegal but also dangerous to approach a black bear, and it is suicidal to approach a grizzly.

CHAPTER 10

Recreationists and Bears

A bear encounter was the last thing on David Reich's mind on the morning of September 16, 1995, as he set out for a short hike in Glacier National Park with his friends Mike Ware and Paul Monteith. Sure, there were bears in the area of Mount Siyeh they planned to hike, but David figured three grown men would discourage any bear. And besides, Mike was carrying some of that new bear-deterrent pepper spray.

As director of human resources at nearby Kalispell Regional Hospital, David found hiking in Glacier to be excellent stress relief, especially the uncrowded Mount Siyeh Trail, where a variety of wildlife such as bighorn sheep and mountain goats adorned the pristine alpine benches like jewels on a crown. Another nice thing about the trail was the fact that they had never seen a grizzly along the way.

About three miles into the hike, the men passed a pond on their right and stopped to discuss eating lunch there. They decided to hike a mile farther and eat on a scenic ridge near Preston Peak. They started hiking again, with Mike in the lead, David in the middle, and Paul at the rear. A hundred yards from the pond, Paul heard brush breaking and looked back to see a large brown grizzly bear burst from the brush near the pond.

"Bear!" Paul yelled. Mike and David whirled to see a grizzly galloping toward them, with a cub following. The men jumped off the trail and each curled into a fetal position. The agitated sow charged up the trail past them.

David Reich recalled, "For a few seconds I thought we were going to be okay because the sow didn't see us lying in the huckleberry brush. Until then, I think she'd just winded us but didn't know where we were.

"But then I heard brush breaking off the trail, and it became obvious that the bear was circling through the brush. I heard a sound behind me and raised my head to see the cub standing just a few feet away."

David jerked his head back down, but the sow spotted the movement. With a furious growl, she charged.

"In the second it took the sow to get there, a flurry of thoughts raced through my mind," David told me. "I knew I was about to be torn into by an angry sow grizzly, and I might be killed. I wondered if I'd ever see my wife and daughter. I had time for one quick prayer to God to let me live long enough to see them again."

The sow pounced on him, raking his back and shoulder with her long claws as she tried to turn him over. At the time, David felt no pain and tried hard not to make any noise, but he grunted a few times as the bear's long claws sunk into his flesh. That seemed to agitate the bear and she tore into him even harder.

Mike Ware wasn't going to lie there and watch his friend endure a mauling. He rose to his knees just fifteen feet away, risking certain attack, and raised his can of bear pepper spray. The sow caught the movement and whirled around in time to catch a face full of bear spray.

David, still conscious and with the huge bear straddling him, looked up as the spray hit the grizzly and watched her begin gagging and whining like a baby. She stood up and wildly pawed at the air in a futile attempt to ward off the sudden pain. She dropped down and turned to leave but swatted David hard on the buttocks before disappearing into the brush with her cub.

Both men helped David to his feet. He assured them that the bear had done little more than rough him up, but as they started back down the trail the adrenaline wore off, and David began to feel pain in his shoulder and back and had trouble walking. They met two other hikers, one of whom was a paramedic who fashioned a rough sling to hold David's injured shoulder and arm in place. By the time the men arrived at the trailhead, David was in great pain, with the first signs of shock setting in. A passing ranger radioed for help and a Kalispell Alert helicopter flew him to the hospital.

David Ware's injuries were far greater than a few scrapes and bruises. The sow grizzly had sunk her claws almost six inches into David's lower back. Fortunately no vital organs were damaged. The risk of infection was great, so doctors didn't stitch up the wounds. However, a friend of David's who practiced acupuncture showed David's wife how to make a poultice from honey and other binding agents that would keep the gaping wounds together while allowing them to drain.

During the healing process, David found it difficult to lie

down for long and spent many sleepless nights pacing the floor to keep his sore back limber. It took three months for David's wounds to heal. An avid swimmer, he was not able to take to the water until mid-December. Five years later, he still has lower back pain. David loves spectator sports but can't sit for more than a half hour, even with a back brace.

"I shudder to think what might have happened if Mike Ware hadn't risked his life to spray that bear," David said. "At the very least, it saved me from even more serious injuries."

Summing up the incident, David said, "We were very fortunate. We actually hiked right past that sow grizzly when we passed the pond. With Mike in the lead, if the bear had attacked him first, we'd have all been at her mercy. I don't have nightmares about it, but the bear's overpowering strength as she knocked me around is still fresh in my mind five years later."

∎ ∎ ∎

David Reich's bear attack could have been much more serious, except for two tactics the hikers employed: they hiked in a group, and one of the men carried pepper spray. These two principles— traveling in a group and carrying pepper spray—have become synonymous with safe travel in bear country.

These two principles also came into play during a bear attack in Canada's Yukon in June 1999 and saved two men from potentially fatal injuries—but just barely.

Phil Vermeyen and his best friend, Ole Ohlson, planned to celebrate Phil's forty-eighth birthday in the wilderness that the California resident loved. They would do it the easy way, paddling by canoe along the Yukon River from Johnson's Crossing, through

Dawson City, and on to Circle City, Alaska. Since the day Phil and Ole had met nineteen years earlier while hiking across the United States, the men had hiked hundreds of miles of wilderness without incident.

The day before their canoe trip began, Ole stopped at a store in Whitehorse, Yukon, to pick up a few camping items. He wandered over to the bear spray and picked up a can of Counter Assault, read the label and the price tag, and almost put it back. During all those years of hiking through some of North America's deepest wilderness, he hadn't needed it. Why waste the money now? On a whim (Ole now laughingly calls it divine intervention), he purchased a can, thinking he'd never need it and rather doubting it would work on an angry bear anyway.

That first evening, the men pulled the canoe out of the Yukon River and onto a beautiful island to camp for the night. After a long day of paddling, they were ravenous and wolfed down a big dinner, followed by a birthday cake that Ole had surprised his friend with. Being experienced backcountry travelers, they kept all food odors out of camp and stashed the food a safe distance away. With a clean camp, and no sign of bears in the area, the men retired to their separate tents thirty feet apart and were lulled to sleep by the mournful wails of loons.

From a deep sleep, Phil Vermeyen jerked awake. "Maybe it was a sixth sense," Phil said, "but I just knew there was a bear in camp. For no obvious reason, I called over to Ole, 'Bear in camp. Bear in camp!'" Ole, sleeping heavily, failed to hear his friend's warning.

"Maybe my voice triggered the bear," Phil said, "because the next thing I know, this huge body smashes into the outside of the tent, biting through the fabric and latching onto my arm. At this point, I'm freaking out. I tried to crawl away, but the bear was on me, biting me in the back, legs, arms."

Ole jumped up as his friend's tent poles snapped and screams ripped through the air. Then came his friend's frantic pleas: "Ole, get the bear off me! Get the bear off me!"

Ole tore into his pack and grabbed the can of bear spray. But he couldn't get the safety tab off. The can was still encased in the heavy plastic shrink-wrapped shroud that keeps the cans displayed in a store from being accidentally discharged. Ole frantically tore off the plastic, released the safety tab, and scrambled out of his tent.

What he saw in the moonlight was his worst nightmare. A huge brown grizzly bear stood over his best friend, clawing and biting at him. Ole strode to within ten feet of the bear. The grizzly stopped and turned toward him. As he raised the can, Ole had the brief thought, *This is as good a day as any to die.* Then he pressed the trigger. The bear jerked backward as the spray engulfed its head, and Phil rolled away. The bear made a move to pounce on the retreating man, but Ole sprayed it again.

With Phil safely out of reach, the bear turned its full attention to Ole, who wondered what to do next—retreat, spray again, or wait for the bear to make a move.

With the grizzly just ten feet away, Ole dared not move, so he hit it with another short burst. The bear didn't back away, so he squirted it again. By now, the can was feeling light, so Ole slowly backed away from the bear to where Phil was kneeling beside the tent. Ole gave his friend a brief hug and helped him to his feet, then he turned back to see what the bear was doing.

The grizzly walked slowly to the fire circle thirty feet away and stood on its hind legs, upper body swaying as it peered balefully at the men. Then it dropped down and walked over to Phil's crumpled tent and sniffed it, threw a surly glance back at the men, and wandered off.

"I could see from the bear's attitude that we were still in a dangerous situation," Ole said. "I had just enough spray left for one more shot, and Phil was bleeding all over the place. I grabbed hold of him to keep him on his feet and said, 'We gotta get out of here fast, Phil, before the bear comes back.'"

Ole was buck naked, and Phil wore only a bloody pair of underwear. "I'm not an exhibitionist," Ole said, "but at the moment, being naked was the least of my worries." He helped Phil into the canoe, then a thought flashed across his mind: *Who's going to help two naked, blood-covered men?* Risking another attack, Ole ran to his tent and grabbed his bag of clothes before shoving off.

With Phil semiconscious and in agony, Ole paddled downstream furiously for eight miles to a cabin at Kirkman Lake. By the time he pulled the canoe ashore, Phil was unconscious. The person in the cabin had a radio and transmitted an emergency call to Dawson City. A helicopter was soon in the air and transported Phil to the Dawson City Nursing Station. His injuries were too severe to be treated there, so he was flown to Whitehorse General Hospital. Ole spent his days at the hospital with Phil, staying in a nearby motel until Phil was released.

Phil is philosophical about the attack. "Last year I hiked all over Australia. Every day I encountered two or three of the most poisonous snakes in the world. I could have died over there just as easily. No, I'm not going to stop doing what I do just because of a single bear attack. But I will carry pepper spray."

Ole sizes up their nightmare by stating, "We had a clean camp.

There was no particular reason for that bear to do what it did. I think it was the old story of predator and prey. We camped in the bear's territory, and he didn't like it, so he set about removing the threat."

"Needless to say," Ole adds, "I'm a bear-spray convert. I doubt I will ever need it again in my lifetime, but one never knows."

■ ■ ■

Folks who combine work with outdoor recreation in bear country sometimes unknowingly put themselves in harm's way. While preoccupied with such chores as picking huckleberries, gathering mushrooms, or collecting shed antlers, they often fail to pay close attention to bear sign or sightings and run the risk of stumbling into a bear. In addition, these outdoor activities often put humans in those specific places where bears are also concentrated, such as berry patches laden with ripe fruit.

Antler gathering is a profitable way to combine work with early-season hiking, especially in areas around Yellowstone National Park. As winter descends upon the mile-high plateau of Yellowstone, about twenty thousand elk migrate from the deep snow in the high country to lower elevations where snow depth is much less. Half the elk herd migrates north to the lowlands near Gardner, Montana. The other half moves south of the park to the bare hills along the Shoshone River north of Cody, Wyoming.

A mature bull elk's antlers can weigh up to thirty pounds and are coveted by artists and craftspeople, who fashion them into everything from rustic furniture to chandeliers. At several dollars per pound, with a premium paid for large sets of matching antlers, many area residents comb the open ridges and meadows in late spring for antlers shed by the elk. In a prime elk wintering area, it's not unusual to find fifty pounds of antlers in a single day.

The areas where the elk herds winter are also places where weak, sick, and old animals routinely die in winter and where cow elk drop their calves. Bears, with only a few blades of grass to eat in spring when they emerge from a long winter of hibernation, descend upon these areas to gorge on carrion and unlucky elk calves.

Cody residents Jeff Buckingham and Cory Nuss had been picking antlers for several years. Both were twenty-year-old soph-omores at the University of Wyoming who depended upon their earnings from antler picking to finance most of their tuition. The young men also looked upon this vigorous endeavor from April through June as a blessed release from the tedium of college class-rooms and long nights of studying.

On a June morning in 1998, Jeff and Cory left the Elks Fork trailhead on the North Fork Shoshone River and hiked briskly into the heart of the elk wintering range. Both men were aware that an occasional grizzly frequented the area. In the past they hadn't worried about it, but in recent years they'd noticed a marked increase in bear sign, so on this trip Jeff carried a .44 magnum pistol. He also brought along a can of bear pepper spray, which he loaned to Cory.

They knew where to look and soon began gathering antlers. Their plan was to pack in as little weight as possible because they expected to be burdened with heavy loads of antlers on the return trip. Consequently, neither man carried a sleeping bag. At dusk that first evening, they huddled under the overhanging branches of a large spruce tree and heated water melted from a snowbank. Dinner would be a few packages of Top Ramen noodles. They spent a miserable night shivering under the tree.

The next day was spent gathering antlers, and at sundown they once more sought the meager protection of a limby spruce tree, with noodles again being the dinner fare. After a long, arduous day hiking the hills, the noodles never tasted better. Cory admits he wasn't crazy about curling up under a tree in bear country, but after two days of roaming over many square miles, they had noticed only one bear track. Still, he slept with his back to the tree trunk.

By midday Sunday, Jeff and Cory were ready to return to the comforts of civilization. An endeavor such as theirs—sleeping under trees in subfreezing temperatures, eating noodles, and struggling under increasingly heavy loads of antlers—would break the average man. But Jeff and Cory were tough and strong and experienced in backcountry survival. For them it was a routine antler-gathering trip. That was about to change.

Staggering under loads that approached a hundred pounds of antlers, they trudged back down the main trail along a creek bottom. With every step closer to the trailhead, their vigilance subsided. In three days they hadn't seen a bear, and both were more than happy to keep it that way.

As they approached a grove of dense timber, Cory looked up and spotted two grizzly cubs fifty yards away. He skidded to a halt and alerted Jeff. Both men stood silently, hoping the cubs would wander off. One of the cubs ambled in their direction, spotted them, and squealed in terror.

A sow grizzly burst out of the timber and stood on her hind legs, swiveling her head and sniffing. The cubs had scrambled past the sow and were running away from the men, so both Cory and Jeff expected the sow to follow after the cubs.

The bear's eyes met Cory's and she immediately charged. "Here she comes!" Cory yelled.

In the seconds that it took the sow to reach them, Cory had time to assess the reality that an enraged grizzly sow was bearing down on them. With their heavy packs, retreat was impossible. In another second, she'd be on them.

The bear picked up speed and came at them low to the ground, teeth bared, ears laid back. She wasn't going to stop. Jeff pulled out his pistol. He'd been preparing for just this sort of thing for years, having rehearsed with his dad what he'd do if charged by a grizzly. Now he had the presence of mind to take a step forward to avoid accidentally shooting Cory, and he leveled the heavy pistol, desperately trying to find the bear in the sights. The sow ran along a gully, and when she was even with them, she lunged up the bank.

Jeff cocked the pistol and was a fraction of a second away from squeezing the trigger when Cory sent a blast of bear spray into the animal's face. The sow stopped at ten feet, staggered backward, then made a U-turn and galloped back to her cubs, gagging and wheezing as she disappeared into the trees.

Cory and Jeff made a wide circle and hustled away, with neither speaking a word for two miles as they put as much distance as they could between themselves and the bear.

"We really weren't scared at the time," Jeff told me the evening we discussed the incident. "Later, when we stopped to rest, that's when we got scared. Knee-knocking scared. What was really freaky about the whole thing was the absence of sound when she attacked. It was as if we were in a well-rehearsed play. For a week after the attack, I'd lie in bed sweating as I relived the incident. I really didn't care if I ever went back in the woods again, but with time, the trauma wore off and I'm back hiking the hills again."

Cory said, "I hope I never see another grizzly that close again.

I think there's getting to be too many of them. They should take them off the endangered species list and allow very limited hunting to put the fear of humans back in them."

Jeff's bear troubles did not end with the grizzly incident. The next spring he and his dad were hiking through a dense stand of timber when they accidentally kicked out a bear. The men were relieved to see it was just a black bear. The animal galloped off and they forgot about it, but a short distance ahead they saw the bear sitting on the hillside seventy yards above, staring at them.

Uncharacteristically, the black bear walked stiff-legged down the mountainside toward them but retreated when they yelled at it. Eventually the bear ignored their yelling and stick throwing and closed to within twenty yards, popping its teeth and making bluff charges. Both men carried bear pepper spray and decided that if the bear moved any closer they would spray it. Though the bear trailed them for another hundred yards, it eventually moved off.

"That taught me a valuable lesson," Jeff said, "because when I first saw it, I thought, *Oh, it's only a black bear.* But that black bear was bigger than the sow grizzly that charged me and Cory."

■ ■ ■

Horseback riding in mountainous country is an outdoor activity that carries its own hazard. A rider runs the risk of serious injury if thrown from the horse. And it sometimes doesn't take much to startle a horse: a mouse scurrying across the trail, or a butterfly fluttering by its nose, or a tree branch brushing across its flank. The smell or sight of a bear is most assuredly a free ticket to a rider's own personal rodeo.

These were facts that Frank Vitail was aware of as he led a string of three pack horses, with one dog, plus two women and one man on horseback close behind. It had been an idyllic summer horseback trip along the North Fork of the Flathead River, a remote strip of wilderness between Glacier National Park and the Canadian border. Each night the group camped along the border, with the awesome peaks of Glacier to the south and the vastness of the Canadian Rockies to the north.

The weather forecast called for gusty winds and rain as a major storm system blew in from the Pacific Coast. Reluctantly, the party decided to leave the high country. As Frank led the group down through alpine meadows, powerful winds buffeted them, and the horses were skittish. They finally dropped down to Two Chuck Ridge, where stunted alpine fir trees afforded a measure of protection from the blustery wind.

Frank saw something ahead that made him forget the wind. The ground on the ridge had been torn up by a bear digging for glacier lily roots. He was about to call back that there might be a bear in the area when he spotted the hump of a bear forty yards ahead. The wind had kept even the loud clopping of the horses from alerting the bear.

Frank's immediate thought was, *Oh man, we're in big trouble.* He knew that if the horses saw or smelled the bear, they'd go nuts. He hastily dismounted and began grabbing reins. He alerted the other riders that a grizzly bear was just ahead and urged them to quickly tether their horses. In the frantic rush that ensued, the bear rose on its hind legs. Two nearby cubs spotted the horses and began crying loudly.

The sow went berserk, bellowing in rage and snarling fiercely. Frank had nothing to stop an attack, but the man behind him carried pepper spray, so Frank grabbed it and turned to face the bear. Every hair on the bear's body was on end as it charged with teeth popping, but at the last second the sow seemed to hesitate, probably because of the madly thrashing horses.

The sow charged again, but the dog dashed past Frank toward the bear. The bear swatted at the suddenly terrified pooch and chased after it off the ridge, leaving her two cubs to wail pitifully. From below the ridge came a tremendous commotion of barking, bawling, bellowing, and brush breaking.

Suddenly a branch snapped behind them, and Frank prepared for a sudden rush from behind. But it was just the dog, returning to cower next to him. Now they had a real problem: they had no idea where the enraged sow was.

"That was the most frightening part of the whole thing," Frank recalled during our interview. "It was like those monster movies. You know it's out there somewhere, but you don't know when or where it's coming from."

Then Frank heard huffing sounds from down the ridge and spun around to see the sow running back to her cubs. Her disposition hadn't improved. She came at Frank again, this time low, with her ears laid back.

At twenty feet he blasted her full in the face. As the red pepper cloud engulfed the bear's head, Frank heard her gagging, and she broke off to the right, shaking her head and gasping for breath as she rounded up her cubs and ran off. That's the last anyone saw of the sow, or anything else for a few minutes, because the gusting wind brought back enough red pepper to set everyone's eyes to smarting.

One of the women was so shaken by the attack that she turned white as a ghost and could barely stand. Not Frank. He found the entire incident invigorating, and he reminded everyone that this was a true wilderness experience that few people ever have.

■ ■ ■

As far as Rich Romano was concerned, bear pepper spray was for wimps. He's a nail-tough Montana cowboy who believed in shooting first and asking questions later—especially when it came to bears. But he had a hankering to ride back into the wild Daly Creek drainage on his trusty horse, Dusty. The problem was that Daly Creek was inside the border of Yellowstone National Park, where firearms are illegal. Honest to a fault, Rich reluctantly left his .44 magnum pistol hanging on a nail and sought an alternative method of self-defense—not for himself, but for his horse, Dusty. After all, a cowboy had to protect his best friend.

Half embarrassed, Rich walked into the Powderhorn Sports Shop in Bozeman, Montana, and sheepishly grabbed a can of UDAP Pepper Power, anxious to get the transaction completed before one of his cowboy buddies saw him with the wimpy stuff.

While Rich drove his pickup down the Gallatin Canyon to the Daly Creek trailhead, a driving rainstorm descended upon the valley. For anyone but a Montana cowboy, it would be ludicrous to leave the warmth of the cab, but Rich simply donned his bibbed rain pants and tied the bear spray to the front of the bib. He threw on a slicker, saddled up Dusty, and went on his way, refreshed by the pounding rain.

Rich was especially enthusiastic about the trip because he'd just purchased a video camera and was looking forward to filming some of the fantastic scenery and wildlife at the head-waters of Daly Creek. Rich stopped several times to shoot video of trees and streams, but so far he hadn't seen any wildlife.

Wouldn't it be nice, he thought, *if I could see a bear and get some video of it.*

A half hour later, he spotted a beautiful creek bottom ahead and turned Dusty off the trail into an idyllic fern glade. The rain had stopped by the time Rich hobbled and tethered Dusty, and it appeared the rest of the day would be glorious, with the sun already breaking through the clouds. Rich sat on a log twenty yards from Dusty and removed his raincoat. He munched a soggy sandwich, rejoicing in the solitude of the secluded creek bottom.

Then Dusty snorted loudly. "What's the matter with you?" Rich called over, but when he saw Dusty's nostrils flared out and his eyes rolling, Rich knew something was wrong. The horse started pulling at the tether rope and whinnying madly.

Rich caught a movement out of the corner of his eye and turned toward it. And gasped. A huge, dark brown grizzly bear stood barely six feet away from him, eyes boring into his. Rich instinctively jumped up, but tripped over his raincoat and fell face first in front of the bear. The grizzly pounced on him, bit into his shirt, and shook him violently.

The bear then swatted him. The huge paw struck Rich in the chest and sent him crashing against a lodgepole pine. For a few seconds, Rich saw stars, felt the blood running down his face, then blackness. When he regained consciousness he was on his back, and the bear was straddling him. Their eyes met, and the bear's look instantly turned to rage. Rich grabbed the bear spray from the holster on the bib strap and flipped off the safety tab. As the bear opened its mouth and lunged, Rich shoved the can into its mouth and sprayed.

The bear leaped into the air and fell backward, gasping and coughing. Then it slowly rolled over and staggered away. Rich stumbled to his feet, bruised and bleeding and ready to get out of there as fast as he could, but one look in Dusty's direction told him he was still in big trouble. Dusty was going berserk, bucking wildly and straining against the tether. *If Dusty breaks away,* Rich reasoned, *no way can I make it ten miles back to the trailhead.*

Rich's heart sank when the tether rope suddenly snapped, but with his front legs still hobbled, Dusty lunged and fell to his knees. Though battered and hurting, Rich seized upon the opportunity and hopped onto Dusty's back a second before the horse regained its legs.

Dusty galloped down the trail like he'd been shot out of a cannon, with Rich holding onto the horse's mane for dear life as a murderous line of trees whizzed by inches away. And then another, more horrifying thought hit Rich: Dusty's hobbles were still on! The horse could, probably would, stumble at any moment, sending Rich flying through the air. By some miracle, Dusty made it a mile down the trail to a meadow, where Rich was able to grab the reins and run the horse in a tight circle until he regained control.

For an hour and a half, Rich rode in pain until he reached the trailhead. He struggled to put Dusty in the trailer, then Rich slid behind the wheel of the pickup and dared to look at his face in the rearview mirror. It was a bloody mess. Rich gingerly wiped the blood away and was relieved to discover that most of his facial wounds were superficial.

"I'm from the old school that says real men don't cry," Rich told me, "but I have to admit that as I sat in that pickup, thinking about how close I'd come to really getting hurt, I burst out crying. Cried like a baby, and I'm not ashamed of it."

He drove up the highway to a pay phone, where he dialed 911 and told the operator that he'd just been mauled by a grizzly bear.

A sheriff's deputy got on the line and told Rich he'd come and get him. "No way would I allow that," Rich said. "I wasn't gonna allow my horse to be left in the middle of nowhere in a trailer. I told the deputy I'd meet him at the town of Big Sky fifty miles up the road. That way someone could take care of Dusty."

Rich Romano's injures proved minor, but he was stiff and sore for weeks, with headaches and earaches for months afterward. "It reminded me of my old rodeo days. I felt like I'd been stomped, which, I guess, I was."

One of the other victims of the bear attack was Rich's lucky shirt. "That shirt survived one marriage and four girlfriends, but the bear ripped it to shreds. I know it sounds strange, but I'd kinda grown attached to it." Fortunately, a lady who heard about Rich's plight offered to make the shirt good as new. Hmmm!

In the true spirit of the Old West, Rich's cowboy friends sent word that they were very happy to hear he'd survived the bear attack—they didn't think he had enough friends to carry the casket and they would have had to go to Bozeman and hire pallbearers. "With friends like that . . . " Rich ruefully mutters while shaking his head.

CHAPTER 11

Anglers and Bears

Within any ecosystem, the bottomland along a stream bank, the riparian zone, serves as a focal point for a variety of wildlife. Rock bluffs and steep mountainsides above often make travel arduous and hazardous. As a result, heavily used game trails can be found meandering along either side of a stream's banks.

Large and small animals, predator and prey, seek out these riparian zones throughout the year for sustenance. In spring, the first shoots of succulent green grass can be found popping up along the stream banks. In summer, when scorching heat dries up the flora elsewhere, riparian zone vegetation flourishes in the damp soil. Come winter, animals such as deer, elk, and moose migrate down to the riparian zone, where snow depth is far less than in the mountains.

While the rest of the animal world ekes out a meager existence during winter, bears hibernate in high mountain dens buried under several feet of snow. By the time a bear groggily emerges in spring, there is usually enough grass below to sustain it until it can find something with more protein.

That protein usually comes in the form of a winter-killed animal carcass or spawned-out fish along the riparian zone. Both grizzly and black bears roam these lowlands seeking flesh, dead or alive. And when they find it, they jealously guard it. An early-season angler, bursting with exuberance to be back on a favorite trout stream after a long winter of inactivity and totally unaware that a bear is guarding a nearby carcass, can easily walk into trouble.

That's exactly what happened to Cody, Wyoming, resident Jeff Shrin in the spring of 1998. Jeff is a vibrant, outgoing member of the band known as Cody! He loves to play and sing the classic tunes of the golden age of rock 'n' roll. But Jeff's life does not revolve around smoky lounges and pounding drumbeats. He readily admits he plays in a band to earn some money to feed his real love—fly-fishing.

Jeff has a passion for the crystal-clear trout streams around Cody, and he gets the shakes if he's not out there every other day. He averages more than a hundred fishing trips a year. In the heat of the summer, he's out there. And when the Wyoming days turn from cool to cold, Jeff can be seen in hip boots sloshing among duck hunters in late October, hoping to get in one more day before freeze-up.

Of all the seasons, Jeff especially enjoys late spring, when the big cutthroat and rainbow trout swim up the pristine tributaries to spawn. It's a short period, when fishing goes from good to awesome, with huge fish taking just about anything offered—a time when fish are measured not in inches but in pounds.

The trout also attract grizzly bears who come to feed on the spawned-out fish. Jeff had been carrying a can of Counter Assault bear spray, but he noticed that the can's expiration date had passed. He stopped at a sporting goods store and discovered a sale on a new discount brand of bear spray. The new stuff, a non-EPA-registered brand, was only half the price of the Counter Assault, so he purchased two cans and walked away, congratulating himself on getting two for the price of one.

On a brisk, clear April morning, Jeff drove to the North Fork Shoshone River about twenty miles south of Yellowstone National Park to partake in this annual rite of spring fishing. As he flipped his own handmade patterns of nymphs and bright, metallic synthetic-roe patterns among the riffles, he occasionally stopped to break the ice away from the eyes on his pole. *Who am I kidding,* he mused. *It'll be another week before the spawn kicks in.* But instead of being disappointed, Jeff was content to wade through the water and luxuriate in the sight of his fly line, a long golden strand, whipping through the sunny spring air.

After an hour of fishing, he'd caught two nice cutthroat, but a gusty wind was wreaking havoc with his casts. He decided to move a half mile to Fishhawk Creek, hoping the steep hillsides would keep the wind down.

He didn't hurry. The old road he trudged along in his chest waders was a well-known grizzly bear highway. Jeff knew from experience that the hours between ten in the morning and four in the afternoon were best for human activity because the bears were usually tunneled back in the brush in daybeds.

In a narrow section of canyon, Jeff located a spot where he could safely scramble down the near-vertical ten-foot cutbank to the boulder-strewn river. In a clatter of raveling rocks, he skidded to the water's edge. The wind was manageable, and he began wading slowly downstream, working each riffle and eddy with his nymphs.

The crunch of rocks across the river came to his ears, but he maintained his concentration on the dark form of a fish following his fly through a small riffle. *Probably just a deer,* he thought, *or maybe an elk. Lots of wintering elk along this creek.* He looked up and gasped.

A huge brown grizzly was lumbering toward him in a purposeful gait. The bear would have to swim to get to him, so he turned and walked out of the water and ran hard for a hundred yards before scrambling up the cutbank and running another hundred yards along the old road.

When Jeff stopped to catch his breath, he mumbled, "Whew! That was close." A second later the big boar lumbered onto the old road, spotted him, and charged.

Jeff had often wondered how he would react if charged by a grizzly. Would he freeze, or run, or act properly? Now, he was struck by the urgency to do everything right, to think clearly and act decisively, to make no mental errors.

He teetered at the edge of the cutbank. It was almost straight down for about ten feet to a jumble of boulders. One glance back at the onrushing bear, and he dove over the edge. He landed on his feet, but when he threw out his hands, he felt a sharp pain in his right wrist and feared he had broken it.

Jeff charged through the willows, sure the bear would be scrambling down at any second. A hundred yards downstream, he spotted a low cutbank and struggled up it. This time he had no illusions that he'd lost the bear. He had to get up a tree, broken wrist and all.

He hurried to a lodgepole pine and tore off his bulky fishing vest. It was then that he remembered the two cans of bear spray. As he pulled the first can from a vest pocket, he accidentally sprayed himself in the face. Blinking away the smarting in his eyes, he mumbled to himself, "I hope this stuff works better than that on a bear!"

The pine tree had no green limbs down low, only a few spindly dead limbs about an inch in diameter. Still wearing waders, Jeff began slowly climbing the tree by hooking his broken wrist over each branch and pulling up. The shock had worn off, and the pain was excruciating every time he used that arm. Eight feet up the tree, he heard a noise and looked to see the grizzly huffing toward him. The bear's determined charge spurred him up the tree another six feet.

The bear stood below, popping its teeth and growling up at him. Jeff balanced precariously on a few dead limbs, worried that one would break at any second, sending him down to those snapping jaws. The grizzly stood up and swiped at him, barely missing his feet.

Jeff took the other can of spray out of his pants pocket and pointed it at the bear's face, barely six feet away. He pulled the trigger, expecting an orange blast of pepper to engulf the bruin. Instead, a weak stream, no greater than bug spray, hissed out of the can.

"It was pathetic," Jeff told me later. "It had absolutely no effect on the bear." Fortunately, the sputtering can dripped enough red pepper into the bear's face that it began coughing and pawing at its eyes. The grizzly finally lumbered back to the riverbank and disappeared over the edge.

Jeff stayed in the tree for half an hour, then climbed down, grabbed his gear, and waddled away. He drove himself to the hospital, and his wrist was operated on within the hour. His girlfriend picked him up and drove him home. On the way to his house, Jeff rubbed his face with his left hand and was instantly blinded by the red pepper residue. His girlfriend ran the red lights in Cody to get him home quickly, where it took twenty minutes of scrubbing to get the pepper off his face and hands.

Investigating authorities surmised that the big grizzly had been roaming along the river, searching for spawned-out trout, but Jeff discounts that theory: "The spawn hadn't even started yet." A few weeks later he learned that some folks had spotted a big grizzly in the same area, feeding on a winter-killed elk. Jeff's guess is that the bear was hidden in the brush across the river, guarding its food cache. He'd hiked right past the bear without disturbing the animal, but the bear was probably alerted when he scrambled down the cutbank.

While Jeff was convalescing, the manager of the Sierra Trading Post in Cody invited Jeff to the store. There, Jeff learned all about good and bad bear sprays, was shown what to look for on a label, and left with a gift of a can of EPA-registered bear spray. "No more cheap stuff for me," Jeff said. "Now I know what to look for on the can."

The wrist healed slowly, and Jeff lost seven weeks of work with the band. Worse than that, he missed the spawning run. With the seriousness of a diehard fisherman, Jeff lamented, "A guy gets only so many cutthroat spawns in his lifetime, you know."

■ ■ ■

The metamorphosis of a bear from a shy, retreating animal to an emboldened predator can happen anywhere food rewards are available. However, the very nature of fishing, which includes smelly fish and their by-products, creates an atmosphere of easy food that is irresistible to a bear.

Brad Brown, a hunting and fishing guide from Red Deer, Alberta, was enjoying a leisurely day off, fly-fishing a small stream north of Banff, Alberta. The trout were rising to an insect hatch brought on by warm midsummer sunlight. Brad had already caught two nice trout, but he hoped to land a big one. In the crystal-clear water, he could see the trout rising in small pools ahead, so he continued wading, casting toward the larger fish.

He came around a bend in the stream, eyes scanning the water across the stream, where a large pool had been created by the upturned roots of a spruce tree. As the fly line whipped through the air, he glanced to his left and was startled to see a large black bear standing in the water along the opposite bank fifty feet away, studying him.

The bear showed neither alarm nor any inclination to leave. Brad Brown knew bears and was well aware of their vagaries of behavior. And he didn't like the baleful look in the bear's eyes. Still, he hoped to defuse the situation by easing back around the bend. The bear suddenly charged across the stream in tremendous splashing leaps.

Who knows what might have happened in the next two seconds, except for the bear pepper spray worn on Brad's belt. Without time to draw it from the holster, Brad shot a two-second burst from the hip and caught the bear full in the face at ten feet. The bear somersaulted backward, thrashed around in the water for a few seconds, then galloped back across the stream. It lay on the opposite bank, wheezing, whining, and vigorously rubbing its face in the dirt.

"I've been around too many bears to trust them," Brad told me. "When you walk into a bear, you have no idea what it's been doing, what kind of day it's had, what kind of food situation it's in, or if there are cubs nearby. It's gotten so I never go anywhere without my pepper spray. All us guides and wranglers who work for Blue Bronna Outfitters carry it. In Canada, we can't carry pistols, and quite frankly, there ain't one man in ten who can hit a charging bear with one."

Brad's habit of carrying bear spray also paid off the next year while he was fishing a stream just north of Waterton Lakes National Park in Canada, the sister park to Glacier National Park in Montana. "I was walking a trail along the banks of the stream, headed for a big pool that's always good fishing, when I walked into a sow grizzly with two cubs. I pulled my pepper spray from its holster while the sow sent her cubs up a tree." (Grizzly cubs can climb trees with no difficulty while their claws are still short enough to dig efficiently into the tree trunk.)

Brad started backing away, but the sow came after him.

"My guess was that it was a false charge, but I was so close to the cubs, I figured no way would I be able to get out of there without something happening, so I sprayed her when she was about thirty feet away."

The sow immediately ran back to the tree that held her cubs, madly rubbing her face with her paws. Brad slowly backed away while the sow brought her cubs down from the tree and rumbled out of sight, shaking her head as she went.

"I'm not a bear magnet," Brad said. "I'm just out there in bear habitat a lot. It's only natural that I'd have a lot more bear encounters than the average person. I'm not foolhardy about it, though. I'll back out of an area if I see a bear ahead, or lots of sign, but sometimes you can't help it when there's a bear suddenly in front of you."

Like the time he drove an ATV around a corner in a trail while traveling to a bowhunting tree stand and surprised a boar grizzly standing in the trail just forty feet away. "The bear made threatening moves toward me," Brad said. "It was obvious that the bear had no intention of leaving the trail. It stood on its hind legs, snapping its jaws and woofing.

"My experience with grizzlies is that when they come down after standing up, they're going to go one way or the other: either away from you or at you. I watched the bear closely, and when he came down he was pointing at me, so I thought a good dose of adverse conditioning might be in order. I sprayed the bear, but a crosswind caught most of the cloud. Enough pepper still reached the bear's snout, though. It jerked its head back and ran about forty yards. It stopped and looked back one more time before diving into the brush."

■ ■ ■

A close-range encounter with an aggressive grizzly is a traumatic event at any time of day, but when it occurs at night, the danger and tension are only magnified. After a long, hard day packing supplies into a backcountry camp, Brad Brown had stretched out inside his tent and fallen into a deep, exhausted sleep. "Suddenly," Brad said, "I was awake. I lay there in that tent, listening. I heard muffled grunts outside, then scraping noises, followed by clinking and banging. I knew it was a bear. It was pitch black in that tent. I didn't know what to do: lay there and hope the bear would go away, or get up and try to scare it off.

"Next thing I know, it's sniffing at the front flap of the tent, and then it pokes its head inside. I could see it silhouetted perfectly in the moonlight. . . . I blasted it in the face with pepper spray. The bear made a choking, gurgling sound and pulled its head out of the tent. Of course, I'd also filled the tent with pepper spray. My eyes burned like fire, and I started coughing and choking.

"Bear or no bear, I dove under the back flap. There I was, howling and coughing behind the tent, and I could hear the bear howling and coughing out front. Finally, I heard it stumble off into the brush. The pepper spray stayed in the tent most of the night, so I had to sleep outside. All in all, it was quite a night."

Another camp incident a few months later had more serious ramifications. About midnight, a coal-black boar grizzly invaded Blue Bronna Outfitters' main camp. Amid a cacophony of barking dogs, stampeding horses, and cursing guides, the big bear tore at the panniers containing horse grain until a guide chased it from camp.

The place had just quieted down when the bear returned and started tearing at bear-proof containers that held the camp food. The cook chased it away, but the bear was back within minutes, slamming around gear and sniffing at tents. The dogs finally chased it a good distance from camp. But a half hour later it was back, this time nosing around the horse corral. Amazingly, the horses banded together and routed the bear.

"This had been going on for hours," Brad said. "When I heard the bear back in camp for the fifth time, I figured, 'Enough is enough.' I grabbed my pepper spray and went after him."

The big grizzly wasn't hard to find. He stood on the other side of the large fire pit situated in the center of the ring of tents, refusing to leave, even with a half dozen men yelling at him. Brad walked up to the other side of the fire pit. A mere twelve feet separated him from 500 pounds of sullen grizzly.

With the other guides' flashlights trained on the bear, Brad shot it full in the face with bear spray. The bear stumbled backward, gagging, and disappeared into the night, coughing and wheezing.

Wildlife authorities arrived two days later with a large baited culvert trap, but the grizzly did not return to the camp. However, that did not end the bear's marauding ways. It crossed a river several miles upstream and raided another outfitter's camp that was empty at the time, but the outfitter and his guides returned while the bear was rummaging in the cook tent. The cornered bear charged and was cut down by a fusillade of gunfire.

One of Brad Brown's favorite black-bear hunting techniques is calling in black bears for hunting clients. When the deer, elk, and moose give birth to their young in spring, the bigger bears turn predatory and roam these birthing areas seeking newborn animals that are too weak to outrun them.

Brad simulates a baby animal in distress by using a predator call device to make loud, squealing sounds. Any mature black bear within hearing usually comes on the run, hoping to catch an easy meal.

"Sometimes the hunter doesn't want to shoot a particular bear," Brad said. "Then it's up to me to run it off. I stand up and wave my arms, and they usually run off, but sometimes they don't. They'll stand there and pop their teeth, determined to drive me from the baby elk or moose they figure is theirs. I've had to spray a few of these bears that just plain refused to go away.

"One time I even sprayed a bear twice. It came toward me, popping its teeth, so I blasted it at thirty feet. When the cloud hit it, the bear started pawing at the air and ran right into a tree.

It fell back and lay there for a second, then it jumped up and ran right at me. I'm sure it was just stunned and disoriented, but I sprayed it again. The bear ran away, squealing like a pig and rubbing its face in the dirt."

Brad shakes his can of bear spray and declares, "I've sprayed two grizzlies and three black bears with this one can of pepper spray. I guess I should go out and buy another one, but it feels like there's enough left in there to take care of another midnight visit from a grizzly."

Brad, buy another can already!

CHAPTER 12

Park Rangers and Bears

Scott Lang looks to be your typical park ranger. Dressed in his official uniform, the thirty-something Lang appears too youthful and clean-cut to fit the image of a woods-wise outdoorsman. But don't let Scott's collegiate air and boyish good looks fool you. He's as tough and as bear wise as anyone in the National Park Service.

Outwalk him? Forget it! As backcountry ranger for the Kintla Lake District in Glacier National Park, Scott hikes anywhere from ten to twenty miles daily for two weeks at a time. (On the day I interviewed Scott at the Polebridge Ranger Station, he'd walked out twelve miles in a driving rainstorm to meet me.)

Scott Lang's woodsmanship is second to none. After fifteen years spent roaming some of the most remote land on the North American continent, he has come to understand the ebb and flow of the cycle of nature; he has seen the cunning pack mentality of the gray wolf on the hunt and the tenacious defiance of the wolverine.

He also knows bears. Intimately. The big ones, the little ones, the four-legged clowns, and the mean ones. Every minute of every day a part of his mind, consciously and subconsciously, studies the deep forest for the slightest perceptible sign—past, present, and future—of bears. The lives of the backcountry recreationists who he monitors are in his hands: that's how he looks at it as he goes about his business of checking on them at wilderness campsites.

In a park where it is illegal for visitors to carry firearms, it would be a contradiction and violation of trust for a park ranger to pack a gun. But Scott Lang is not defenseless. He uses his woodsmanship to avoid bear trouble. But if you spend enough time in the backcountry, bear expert or not, you're going to find yourself face-to-face with an aggressive bear. For those blue-moon occasions, Scott Lang carries bear pepper spray.

One of Scott's closest calls with a grizzly came as the result of a slight oversight on his part. He was hiking the length of a trail to make sure no other people were on it in advance of closing the trail because a sow grizzly and cubs were reported in the area. Scott made lots of loud talk as he walked: "Hey bear! Hey bear!" He finally arrived at the end of the trail, having met no other hikers. With the trail clear, he turned back, his long legs sending him at a brisk pace down the steep path.

Fifty yards along the trail, he rounded a bend and walked right into the sow and two cubs. The sow bluff-charged him once, then again. Now just twenty yards away, the sow began popping her teeth and bouncing stiff-legged toward him. Scott spoke to the bear in a low voice and slowly backed away.

The sow seemed content to avoid a confrontation, but when Scott pulled loose the Velcro flap that covered the pepper spray on his hip holster, the loud tearing sound sent the sow into hysterics. She bounced stiff-legged toward him, clacking her teeth and making bluff charges. His finger gripped the trigger on the can of spray, and he made the conscious decision that if the sow came one step closer, he'd blast her. Seconds passed like hours as the furious sow grizzly and trembling park ranger stood mere feet from each other on that isolated trail.

The sow slowly turned away, took a few steps, and glanced back. Scott remained motionless. The sow walked back down the trail with her cubs for fifty yards, stopping several times to eye her interloper, before turning uphill.

"It was tense for a while," Scott said. "Real tense. After it was over, I could have kicked myself for getting into that predicament. I let my guard down for a couple minutes because I'd just walked by that place sixty seconds earlier yelling my lungs out, so I figured any bear in the area would have heard me. I learned two valuable lessons that day: take nothing for granted in bear country, and pull the Velcro loose before the bear gets in my face."

Scott's most dangerous encounter, forcing him to use pepper spray to avoid a mauling, occurred with a black bear. It was late July 1998, and Scott was hiking up the Kintla Lake Trail when he came around a corner in a brushy section of the route and surprised a 150-pound black bear.

Scott yelled and waved his arms, and the bear ran up the trail, but it stopped fifty yards away and turned back to reassess the situation. "At that point," Scott said, "I had no inkling the encounter would escalate into a life-threatening incident. I'd run into lots of black bears, and most ran away when they identified me as a human. But this bear was different. As soon as it turned back toward me, I just knew it would be different."

Scott took two steps forward and aggressively confronted the bear, bellowing at the top of his voice and gesturing wildly. That seemed to intimidate the bear, and it backed up, then loped into the brush above the trail. All was quiet for a minute, and Scott thought it was all over. He was about to continue on, when the bear suddenly jumped onto the trail just twenty yards away, this time with its hackles up and baleful eyes on him.

"With that bear looking directly at me," Scott said, "I knew I wasn't going to get out of this thing by yelling. The bear had a real aggressive look to him, like he'd thought it over and decided that I was nothing to fear. I backed down the trail, but the bear kept coming. Then the thought flashed through my mind: *Maybe if I stepped off the trail, the bear might walk past me.*"

Scott retreated behind a tree about ten yards below the trail. "For a few minutes the forest was silent," Scott said, "and I thought maybe the bear had wandered off, what with me being out of his sight. The bear suddenly charged down the trail, stopped in front of me, and came at me in a stiff-legged gait.

"That bear acted like no other black bear I've ever seen. It was swaggering and popping its teeth and growling. I backed behind the root wad of a big spruce blowdown. A second later the bear leaped onto the top of the roots. It looked down at me, gnashing its teeth. At that point, it was just eight feet away, and I knew that if I didn't do something immediately, it would be on me."

Scott shot the bear in the face with a long blast of bear spray. The animal somersaulted backward and hit the ground hard, bawling and pawing at its face. It jumped up and ran into a tree trunk, which seemed to stun it because it lay on the ground for a few seconds before regaining its feet. The bear then tried to climb the tree but couldn't because it kept pawing at its face. Finally it slid to the ground and bolted into the brush above the trail.

"Those three-year-old black bears are unpredictable," Scott said. "They've been chased away by the sow because they're big enough to fend for themselves. Then the big boars rout them from their territory, so they're looking to stake out a place of their own. Sometimes they'll pull dumb stunts like that."

They'll also pull dumb stunts that get them killed. Scott said that a few weeks later another ranger found a dead black bear along the same stretch of trail. Scott hiked in to investigate and found where a very large, powerful animal had literally picked up the 150-pound black bear's carcass and carried it to a rock bluff forty yards above the trail.

"I couldn't be positive because of the ravaged condition of the carcass," Scott said, "but I think it was the same bear. My guess is that it ran into a grizzly and was dumb enough to stand its ground."

■ ■ ■

To the casual observer, the position of park ranger is a dream job, getting paid to spend days upon days hiking through some of America's most spectacular wilderness as you perform your exalted duty of preserving and protecting the park's inhabitants and visitors.

But a ranger's job is not for everyone. While cordially dealing with the wide-eyed public, a ranger must also possess a mental toughness, bordering on combat readiness, because at any moment his or her life may be on the line. And oftentimes a bear/human conflict is at the root of the problem.

Glacier Park ranger Paul Downey's moment of destiny began to unfold on July 20, 1998, when he responded to reports of a large sow grizzly and two cubs frequenting the trail to Iceberg Lake in the Many Glacier area. Downey hurried up the trail, anxious to study the bear and decide if it was being aggressive.

Four miles in, Downey spotted the light brown sow with one dark and one light cub. The animals were feeding on frost-burnt huckleberries. Of most concern to Downey was a lone boar grizzly about 250 yards above the trail. The potential was great that the boar might eventually try to get at the cubs, and that would enrage the sow. And an enraged sow was unpredictable and dangerous.

The next day he received a report that a hiker on the Iceberg Lake Trail, traveling alone and making no noise, had come around a bend and looked up to see the sow charging him. Rather than drop to the ground and play dead, the man ran back down the trail for two hundred feet. Miraculously, the sow aborted her charge. The terrified man waited for half an hour until a large group of hikers came by, and he joined them. Amazingly, some say foolishly, the group slipped without incident past the sow and her two cubs as they fed just twenty-five feet below the trail.

Downey immediately hiked up the trail and spotted the sow and cubs a hundred yards above the trail. The bears ignored his loud yelling but finally moved into the krummholz (stunted subalpine fir). One more incident, Downey's supervisor informed him, and he was to close the Iceberg Lake Trail. They would then have to deal with the sow or wait until she moved to a less busy area of the park

On July 25, hikers reported that the sow and cubs had followed them for several hundred yards down the Iceberg Lake Trail. Anxious to avert a tragedy, Downey started up the seven-mile-

long trail that afternoon in order to close it. He planned to post
signs saying, "Trail Closed Ahead Due to Bear Danger."

Yelling "Hey Bear!" every few seconds as he walked, Downey
strung parachute cord and a sign across the trail at the junction
of the Many Glacier horse trail and the spur that runs back to the
parking lot at the Swiftcurrent Motor Inn. As he moved up the
trail, he found fresh bear scat and a recently overturned log with
termites still crawling over it.

Near Iceberg Lake, Downey was relieved to finally spot the
sow and cubs on the trail a hundred yards away. At least now he
knew where they were. He yelled and yelled, but the bears refused
to leave the trail. After ten minutes of yelling, the sow cast a
nettled look his way and grudgingly stepped off the trail. In
Downey's eyes, the sow was clearly in no mood to react peaceably
to any unknowing hiker who might come down from one of the
trails that fed into the Iceberg Lake Trail from above. Downey
had to somehow reach the trail's terminus three miles away as
soon as possible and shut the trail down.

Downey made a wide circle above the bears through dense
krummholz and over rock ledges. The detour cost him an hour,
but he figured he still had enough time to close the trail and make
the return hike to the parking lot at Swiftcurrent Motor Inn before
dark. Back on the trail, he hurried ahead, yelling loudly as he went,
but he saw no other bears. He stretched parachute cord across the
trail and hung a "Closed" sign, then hurried back down the trail.
Near Iceberg Lake, he looked ahead and his heart sank. The sow
and cubs were back near the trail.

With the surly bear a hundred yards ahead, he didn't dare
proceed, but the sun was dipping close to the horizon. He again
circled above the bears through rugged terrain. It was almost an

hour before he made it back to the trail about four hundred yards below the area where the bears had been last seen.

In waning light, Downey hiked briskly along the trail, still clapping and yelling every few seconds, "Hey bear! Hey bear!" Suddenly, he heard a loud series of snarls coming from dense cover about a hundred feet below the trail. Downey yelled even louder now, making sure the bear knew he was a human. The sow responded with threatening growls.

Downey's heart thumped loudly as he watched the five-foot-tall brush part and saw the bear barrel through it toward him. The bear's bellowing intensified, and the crashing in the brush increased until it was a steady roar. Downey pulled his can of bear spray from its hip holster, but he realized he had a serious problem. The dense brush grew to within ten feet of the trail. He wouldn't have the luxury of laying down a protective cloud of pepper spray at long range. Anything that went down in the next few seconds would be at point-blank range.

Adrenaline flooded his body, intensifying every instinct and conscious thought until the entire scenario unfolded as if in slow motion. The sow burst into the open about twelve feet to his right. Her eyes locked onto his, and she lunged at him. Downey dodged to the left, putting a few feet between himself and the bear, and sprayed her at ten feet. The bear's head jerked backward, but she continued paralleling toward him from below the trail.

Downey sprayed as he retreated, catching the sow full in the face for almost four seconds. The bear slowed her charge, then stopped as she was overcome by the red pepper. She emitted a gurgling gasp, whirled, and dove back into the brush.

Downey hurried down the trail through the twilight. He radioed to ranger headquarters that he'd just been charged by the sow and had used up most of his can of spray. Four rangers congregated at the trailhead to dash up the trail and rescue their comrade, just as Downey arrived there.

The trail remained closed while rangers monitored the area. With her newfound respect for humans, administered as a dose of aversive conditioning from Downey's bear spray, the sow left the congested Iceberg Lake area. A week later, the trail was reopened.

■ ■ ■

For all the pleasure and satisfaction that marks a park ranger's life, there are at least two distasteful chores associated with the profession: packing out bear-attack victims and killing bears. These grim jobs require more than youthful courage and savvy. It takes men and women with enough experience and fortitude to function while staring at the partial remains of a human body or to look through a rifle scope at a grizzly and squeeze the trigger on an animal they have sworn to protect. These chores fall to a small core of seasoned veterans who have reached Level Four bear management—dealing with death. Level Four gives a ranger the dubious honor of killing a grizzly when necessary.

It's not only discouraging and depressing, but it's also dangerous, as rangers John Lounsbury and Mona Divine learned in 1987 when they responded to a call about a car parked illegally at a campground near Canyon in Yellowstone National Park. The car belonged to photographer Bill Tesinsky. Lounsbury knew that a habituated grizzly had been loitering in that area. As Lounsbury and Divine began a zigzag search away from the road, Lounsbury hoped for the best but expected the worst.

Anyone familiar with the woods knows that the raven is a

harbinger of death, so when a single raven croaked from its perch in a red fir tree, Lounsbury, in the lead, advanced cautiously in that direction. What he saw in a small draw sent a chill up his spine. A grizzly bear was feeding on something just twenty-five yards ahead. He'd almost walked right into the bear. The rangers eased back out of sight, then hurried to their vehicle and returned with a pair of binoculars for a closer inspection. Lounsbury also brought along a high-powered rifle.

One glance through the binoculars told Lounsbury all he needed to know. The bear lay on a mound of scraped-up dirt, feeding on a leg. At the end of that leg was a tennis shoe. The rangers again hurried back to their vehicle and radioed to the other searchers that they had found Bill Tesinsky's remains. They then radioed to park headquarters to apprise them of the situation. A quick, terse reply was forthcoming: kill the bear.

With a party of other rangers as backup, two men armed with rifles eased forward in good shooting light and placed the crosshairs of their telescopic sights on the shoulder of the bear as it fed on Tesinsky's remains. Both rifles roared simultaneously, and the bear dropped.

Then it was the chore of the search party to round up the parts of Tesinsky that could be found. After three days, the bear had eviscerated the body and cut it in half, burying huge chunks of bone and muscle in hastily dug holes. The rest it had eaten.

National park policy is deceptively simple. Any bear that kills and feeds on a human must be killed. However, this policy evolved from many hard days spent wrestling with issues such as these: What if a bear is feeding on a human carcass, but you don't know if the bear had killed the person? What if other predators, such as mountain lions and wolves, are present?

These cases where evidence of predation on a human is unclear are handled on a case-by-case basis. But to allow a bear to live, after killing a human and then eating the flesh, opens up a lot of possibilities—all of them bad. In the Tesinsky case, the proof was irrefutable, and the bear was killed.

Every ranger acted efficiently and professionally throughout the ordeal, and the site was cleaned up of bear and human remains within hours. I guess you could call it a job well done, but I doubt you'd get any of those men and women to look at it that way. There were too many doubts, too many questions. For example, is it fair to kill an animal who simply responded to a human's intentional intrusion into its safety zone, as Bill Tesinsky had done when he approached to photograph the feeding grizzly? In the end, the decision was made against that bear because of the Park Service's responsibility to also protect the visiting public from an animal who might want to try it again after discovering that people are good to eat.

■ ■ ■

While the discovery of Bill Tesinsky's body and the subsequent elimination of the bear that killed and ate him were completed within hours, rangers in Glacier National Park were not so fortunate when they responded to the disappearance of twenty-six-year-old Craig Dahl in 1998.

Dahl, a park employee, had gone on a day hike. Search parties the next day failed to find any sign of him, then two days of sleet and snow made searching impossible. Dahl had been missing for three days when rangers arrived with two bloodhounds at the Mount Henry/Scenic Point parking lot, where his vehicle was parked. Due to steady snowmelt and the heavy rain and snow that had fallen, the hounds were almost worthless.

Approaching darkness kept rangers from proceeding with the search that evening, but the next morning six search teams and a helicopter were sent out to look for Dahl. And then Blackfeet tribal biologist Dan Carney, who was assisting in the search, got some disturbing signals from his radio transmitter. The signal came from a radio-collared grizzly with two large cubs, and it was coming from the search area.

That changed the entire complexion of the operation: a missing hiker and a grizzly bear in the same area. Could be just a coincidence, but probably not.

Searchers found old tracks that looked human, and three sets of tracks that appeared to be made by bears. The human tracks cut downhill across three switchbacks in the trail, with the bear tracks following. Then the snow ran out and so did the trail. Rangers followed the general direction of the tracks and made the grisly discovery of Craig Dahl's partially consumed body below a series of small rock ledges. The fact that both Dahl and the bears ran over the snowfield lent credence to the conclusion that the bears reacted to Dahl's running away by chasing after him.

An investigation team was sent in, along with a security squad of eight armed rangers to protect the perimeter in case the bear returned to its food cache. Bear scat and hair samples were taken and flown to the University of Idaho for DNA testing to make sure the radio-collared bear, known as Chocolate Legs, was indeed the killer of Craig Dahl. (Hair samples had been taken from Chocolate Legs when she had been previously live-trapped.)

The popular Two Medicine area was closed to all visitor traffic. For the next two days, rangers played a hectic game of cat and mouse with Chocolate Legs and her two cubs as they tried to keep tabs on the bears. On the third day, rangers Tim Peach and Joe Manley, both armed with shotguns, and biologist Carney located the bears at the footbridge that crosses Two Medicine Creek. The armed men had the bears just 150 feet away and could have easily eliminated the entire family at that point, but until the DNA testing came back, Chocolate Legs was only a suspect. They chased the bears away from the bridge by firing cracker shells, which burst upon impact and frighten bears.

It took a week for the DNA results to come back. Chocolate Legs was indeed the killer and scavenger of Craig Dahl. The decision was made to kill Chocolate Legs and her two cubs, and rangers hustled to get it over with quickly. Then misfortune struck.

With the breeding season beginning, a large, dark boar grizzly had descended upon the condemned family and chased both sub-adult bears off. Chocolate Legs was seen in the company of the large boar on the slopes above upper Two Medicine Valley, but both bears disappeared before rangers arrived. Baited foot snares were strung out through the lake area.

But time was running out for Chocolate Legs. Unlike her two offspring, who could escape into the dense cover, Chocolate Legs was wearing a radio collar that betrayed her whereabouts. On May 30, she was located by telemetry and then spotted from the air in an avalanche chute with the big boar, but she again disappeared before rangers arrived.

On June 2, a female cub was caught in a foot snare, tranquilized with a drug, and placed in a cage trap. Rangers were now faced with a dilemma. While the cubs were with Chocolate Legs, their identity was obvious, but now, rangers had no way of knowing if the young female in the trap belonged to Chocolate Legs. They were forced to take a hair sample and rush it to the University of Idaho for DNA testing. In the meantime, they tried to use the cub as a lure in hopes of bringing in Chocolate Legs and the other sibling.

On June 4, Chocolate Legs was again located by telemetry, and this time she was alone, foraging near No Name Lake. Rangers shot and killed her. The next day DNA results positively linked the female cub to Chocolate Legs. It was tranquilized and shot. And still it was not over. The other cub had to be found.

The second cub proved elusive. Rangers scoured the vast expanses of rugged terrain for more than a week without finding the young bear. Their job became increasingly difficult because more bears were showing up daily as the valley greened up and more tourists descended upon the beautiful Two Medicine Valley. After one last massive sweep by armed rangers, the Two Medicine area was reopened to tourists on June 11.

Two weeks later, rangers received a report of a sub-adult grizzly charging hikers near the pit toilets in upper Two Medicine Valley. Chances were good that it was the bear they were looking for. Four teams of rangers spread out to look for it. Two hours later, rangers Chuck Cameron and Dick Mattson spotted the young bear in an avalanche chute above Two Medicine Lake. The men hurried up the steep slope, until they could see the bear 150 yards away.

But now they had to positively identify the young bear as one of the bears that had scavenged Craig Dahl's body. This bear was supposed to have a tarnished silver tag in its right ear. After ranger Cameron identified the ear tag through a spotting scope, ranger Mattson shot the bear from a distance of eighty yards.

After more than a month of armed patrols, human body parts, and dead bears, it was finally over. The Two Medicine Valley returned to normal, with hikers again traversing trails, anglers catching the native cutthroat trout, and kids splashing in the lake. The cost had been staggering, and thousands of worker hours had been expended. But if rangers expected a pat on the back for a tough job well done, they would be disappointed. A new storm arose when some bear experts questioned whether Chocolate Legs was Craig Dahl's killer.

Chuck Jonkel, a respected bear biologist, stated, "Just because the bear scavenged the carcass doesn't mean she killed Craig Dahl. There were other bears in the area, as well. Any bear that finds a dead body, animal or human, considers it edible carrion. In my opinion, there just wasn't enough evidence to remove that bear and her cubs from the ecosystem."

But others supported the park's actions. Chris Servheen, grizzly bear recovery coordinator for the U.S. Fish and Wildlife Service, said, "The evidence was clear. That bear, known as Chocolate Legs, pursued Craig Dahl. It ran him down and killed him, and then the entire family fed on the body. That bear and its cubs had to be taken out."

■ ■ ■

Chief Ranger Charlie Logan takes such controversy and second-guessing in stride. After thirty years as a ranger, the man in charge of the entire western half of Glacier National Park isn't easily ruffled. It's the dead bodies and mutilated victims that bother him—and the times when he has had to put his Level Four status to use and kill a grizzly.

"It's hard," Charlie told me. "I have the best job in the world, but its downside takes you way down. It doesn't happen often, but I've had to pack out people who were horribly injured by bears, and when a bear steps over the line, I have to kill it. It goes against everything I'm here to do."

Charlie shakes his head and laments, "Bears get fed by people. They get habituated and lose their fear of humans, and then we have to kill them. I really hate it. I don't think you can ever make the potential danger go away in bear country, but if people would just get educated on bear behavior a little bit before they come here, there would be less personal injury and a whole lot less bear trouble.

"I push pepper spray all the time. I always carry the stuff, and I hand out our position paper on pepper spray that explains what to look for in a pepper spray and why you should carry it. And still, people don't carry the stuff. I don't know how people can walk right by a ranger carrying bear spray prominently displayed on his belt and then waltz out into grizzly country without it."

CHAPTER 13

Stopping Other Large Predators

B ear deterrent pepper spray is manufactured solely for the purpose of stopping a bear attack, and all EPA-registered sprays are required to label their products as such. However, individuals have used bear spray, with its maximum-strength formula, to deter other large-animal attacks, and some of these incidents are worth noting.

■ ■ ■

Next to the bear, the mountain lion is the largest predator roaming the western United States and Canada. Females average about 120 pounds, while mature males weigh up to 200 pounds. They are extremely efficient hunters. They use stealth and lightning-quick speed to catch and kill animals much larger than themselves, such as 800-pound elk and half-ton moose, though their main prey is deer.

While the total grizzly population in the western states is only about thirteen hundred, there are tens of thousands of mountain lions in the West, with their numbers and range growing because of an increase in the deer population and because voters in California and Washington have banned mountain lion hunting. And unlike the grizzly, whose preferred habitat is the remote wilderness, a lion can be found anywhere there's a base of prey, such as deer.

The rise in lion numbers has spawned a corresponding increase in lion attacks on humans. In California, about a dozen people are attacked by mountain lions every year. So great has the lion population swelled in that state that about two hundred lions are killed annually by motor vehicles.

One chilling aspect to the increase in these numbers is the fact mountain lions' human prey is often a child. In 1989 a lion attacked and killed a child while he was playing in his backyard in a rural subdivision in Montana. Another young person was killed while hiking a popular trail with his family in Rocky Mountain National Park. In 1998 a ten-year-old boy was dragged away from a large group of youths on a summer camp outing in Montana. Only the quick action of the group leader, who pummeled the cat with his fists, saved the boy's life.

I've had several encounters with mountain lions because I'm in the woods so often, but my most unsettling encounter occurred only a few hundred feet from a county road in Montana. I'd just left my pickup to take a midwinter hike along a creek-bottom trail when I spotted a large mountain lion slinking through the underbrush parallel to the trail. At first I thought it had failed to see or hear me because of the dense cover and the roaring creek nearby. But when I stopped, the lion stopped; when I moved, it moved.

I lost sight of the big cat, but then it crossed the trail forty yards in front of me. The longer I walked, the bolder the lion became. Finally the lion loped out of sight, and I hoped that was the end of it.

A sharp bend in the trail lay ahead. It was an excellent place for an ambush. I tentatively approached the corner, hoping for the best but expecting the worst. I got the worst. The lion lay crouched beside a log thirty feet from the trail, waiting. His ears were laid back, and his tail twitched back and forth.

I knew if I traveled lion country long enough, I'd find myself in exactly this type of predicament, so I'd begun carrying bear pepper spray even in winter.

I slowly raised the can. The lion tensed, legs bunched, ready to spring. A loud blast of spray shot forward and engulfed the cat in a huge orange ball. The startled cat leaped six feet into the air, snarling and pawing wildly at the air. It hit the ground and disappeared into the forest in a blur.

Canadian hunting and fishing guide Brad Brown told me that he also thwarted a mountain lion attack with bear pepper spray. While on a summer horseback trip, Brad noticed that the horses were acting edgy as he led them along a creek-side trail hemmed in by a rock cliff. Brad looked up and spotted a large lion crouched on a ledge twelve feet above. The lion hungrily eyed the horses behind Brad, so he pulled out his bear spray and blasted it. "I don't know whether it was the pepper spray or the loud noise, but that cat took off so fast it was just a brown streak."

Many wildlife officials, park personnel, and biologists suggest that travelers in lion country should carry bear pepper spray. In addition, anyone living in known lion habitat should keep bear spray readily available, and they should teach their children how to use it in an emergency. And here's the good news: while a bear may take a lot of spraying to deter an attack, a mountain lion is quickly unnerved by the spray's loud noise, and a lion's nose and eyes are extremely sensitive to pepper spray.

■ ■ ■

In the jungles of Africa and Asia, native peoples either aren't allowed to carry a high-powered rifle or simply can't afford one. In the future, bear pepper spray may be found in every native's waist-band for defense against dangerous animals ranging from lions and tigers to hippos and hyenas.

Mark Matheny of UDAP received the following letter from Bhagavan Antle, director of TIGERS, the Institute of Greatly Endangered and Rare Species, in India.

> Sir, I have used your UDAP Pepper Power for the control of big cats as a non-lethal and non-physically damaging method of stopping these powerful animals from hurting each other. Below are a few examples of your spray being put to good use:
>
> One day a large male tiger was brought into the cage of a female for the purpose of breeding. However, the male grabbed the female by the throat and maintained its death grip on her even after the use of CO_2, water hoses and loud noise. Finally, we gave the male tiger a short blast of Pepper Power from about twenty feet. The male tiger immediately released the female and ran to a corner.
>
> Another time, we had several male African lions out in the compound together when one male bit another on the tail. The bitten male spun around and attacked the other lion. I was standing

thirty feet away, and it became obvious that these two lions would inflict serious damage to each other. I sprayed the fighting lions, and the animals stopped immediately, with little injury from the fight.

Carl Mogenson, director of Natural Bridge Zoo in Virginia, also endorses the use of bear pepper spray as a deterrent for big cats. He used it to save the life of one of the tigers at the zoo after the exhibit that houses a pair of tigers had another female introduced.

"All went well for a week," Mogenson said in a letter to Mark Matheny, "until the male tiger suddenly attacked the new female, clamping its jaws over the side of her head, while the other female grabbed her by the leg. The male had a death grip on the new tiger."

Mogenson sprayed both attacking animals with a short burst of bear spray, and they immediately stopped the attack. The injured female tiger recovered, and Mogenson said the three animals began getting along much better.

"I have been in the zoo business for thirty-five years," Mogenson said, "and I feel pepper spray has a very powerful and immediate effect upon wild felines when situations of harm arise. This product stops the animals in their tracks with no lasting harmful effects."

■ ■ ■

Vicious dogs are responsible for more serious injuries and deaths to humans every year than bears and mountain lions combined. It is unnerving for a casual stroller, far from the lairs of wilderness predators, to find himself the object of a vicious animal attack.

Such was the case when Richard Boulware took his little Scottish terrier, Angus, for an evening walk in a suburb of Denver, Colorado.

Worried that he or his dog might be attacked by aggressive dogs, Boulware began carrying pepper spray. As Richard and Angus sauntered around a corner, they were confronted by two eighty-pound dogs that charged them with threatening snarls and bared teeth.

"With only seconds to react, I yanked my Scottie into my arms while simultaneously drawing my pepper spray from my waistband," Richard said. "As the two big dogs closed in for the attack, I sprayed. They stopped like they'd hit a brick wall! Last seen, the two dogs were turning somersaults and rubbing their muzzles in the grass."

■ ■ ■

The only place the grizzly bear can be found in California these days is on the state flag, the species having been exterminated there in the 1800s. But that doesn't mean there aren't some big ornery animals to deal with, especially if you're a veterinarian.

Andrew Borrowman works exclusively with cattle in the Chino area of southern California, where more than one hundred thousand dairy cows and bulls are tended to by a core of vets who often risk their lives when dealing with the short-tempered bulls.

"These bulls can weigh up to two thousand pounds and are extremely dangerous," Borrowman said in a letter to Mark Matheny. "You can never let your guard down when you're near one."

Borrowman said the nature of his work forces him to occasionally turn his back on a bull, so he began carrying bear spray. "If I'm not carrying it, I feel naked," he said. "Whenever a bull crosses the line from threatening to dangerous, I let him have it with bear spray. It takes the wind right out of his sails."

■ ■ ■

If you think a charging, three-hundred-pound grizzly is scary, just imagine what it would be like to face six tons of bellowing, rampaging elephant! That's the terrifying predicament many African and Indian farmers face when they try to stop marauding elephants from ravaging their crops.

You can't blame the elephants. Their shrinking range and enormous appetites, requiring 900 pounds of forage per day, often force them to invade agricultural areas and dine on field crops.

And you can't blame the farmers. Picture the damage a dozen ravenous elephants can do to a cornfield during one raid. Faced with the prospect of famine, frustrated farmers have resorted to clanging pots and pans in an effort to chase the elephants away. But these lumbering pachyderms don't scare easily, and they don't like being startled. In Zimbabwe alone, elephants trample to death about twelve farmers annually. During a rampage in Nigeria, rogue elephants destroyed vast tracts of crops on forty-four farms in the state of Borno, and during this rampage three farmers were trampled to death.

It would be suicidal to walk within thirty yards of an elephant and attempt to stop it with a twelve-ounce can of bear pepper spray. Something with a much larger carrying capacity and range is needed.

The *Economist* newspaper reported that, in an effort to save the elephants and the farmers, Oski Osborn, a student of elephants who is based at the University of Cambridge, England, has been experimenting with pepper spray to force elephants off croplands. After working with various delivery systems, he developed an elephant-deterrent system that employs a large canister of pepper spray shot mortar style from a high-powered rifle. The canister releases its capsicum over the field, and it settles over the entire elephant herd, sending the elephants coughing, sneezing, and bellowing for the safety of the deep forest.

The elephant spray kit, containing refillable pepper spray canis- ters, pepper spray, and cleanup gear—costs about seven hundred dollars. This price is too much for the average farmer, but an entire village might be able to afford a single unit to be used by its farmers collectively. Osborn hopes that increased demand will appreciably lower the cost of an elephant pepper spray kit.

This unique use of pepper spray may yet become one of the greatest conservation tools for protecting the elephant, because the only alternative for frustrated farmers and authorities is to kill the trespassing animals.

■ ■ ■

Pepper spray, in its extremely potent bear-deterrent form, should not be used against humans for self-defense. Two men died in recent years when they were subdued by Montreal police using pepper spray, even though it was the weaker police-grade spray. One of the men was an asthmatic, but the other casualty had no known medical conditions, such as asthma or a weak heart.

Personal-defense pepper spray is sold in diluted form in a smaller can, and it can work very well against a human attacker, as Elizabeth Herdina of Vancouver, Washington, found out. She had purchased a key-chain-size, half-ounce can of self-defense pepper spray just weeks before the time she returned to her apartment and discovered a burglar at work.

The man stood six feet, three inches tall and weighed well over two hundred pounds. As soon as he saw the frightened woman, he rushed her. Elizabeth dropped her groceries and pulled out her key-chain pepper spray. She sprayed the intruder as he grabbed her.

The man pawed at his face, howling, and fell to the floor. Elizabeth ran outside and waved down a deputy sheriff driving by on night patrol. The deputy found the intruder still on the floor, writhing in pain.

An important note: Never carry a small, personal-defense pepper spray for protection against a bear!

CHAPTER 14

The Return of the Great Bear

I t is unnerving to some people, in this age of such amazing human accomplishments as digital computing and genetic breakthroughs, that there are still places where humans remain subordinate to a lumbering quarter ton of taut muscle and silver-tipped fur, to an animal that is exponentially bigger, stronger, and faster.

For this reason, some folks fear the return of the great bear. They fear being attacked and argue that a single human injury is unacceptable. That line of thinking is less persuasive when you consider that dogs kill more than a dozen people each year; that we annually slaughter thousands of members of our own species with automobiles; and that over the past few decades, only about one person per year has been killed by a bear.

And yet, this fear is understandable when we trek through grizzly country, for we are suddenly forced to conform to a new standard of behavior, where survival is awarded to the swift, the strong, the cunning; where might usually triumphs; and where there is no right or wrong. The roles have been reversed, and all our mastery of megabytes and DNA is trivial when compared with the power of the great bear's bite.

Surprisingly, these primal conditions lure people from all walks of life—lawyers and housewives, bankers and grocery clerks—into the wilderness, where they tread softly, hesitantly, carefully for the chance, however remote, of catching a glimpse of the mighty grizzly bear. Many of these enthusiasts, myself included, are seeking a piece of human essence that has been lost. While the grizzly has retained its taciturn, stately being, we have evolved into cerebral superiority, eroding in certain ways into physical and personal flaccidness. We strive to commune with the great bear, however briefly, because the grizzly mirrors some of what we as a species once were: noble, resolute, cunning.

Ultimately, public opinion will decide whether the grizzly will return to any of its former haunts. A century ago, almost all of the fifty thousand grizzlies in the continental United States were slaughtered in a shameful program of elimination. Today the scales have tipped, with polls indicating that as many as 80 percent of Americans favor the grizzly's return to suitable areas in its former range. That says something for our humanity—that so many people support the presence of a fellow creature that is in some ways superior to us.

The future of the grizzly bear in the western United States is currently a tale of good news and bad news. Thanks to the protection afforded by the Endangered Species Act and better bear management, grizzly numbers have increased in the past decade. The Yellowstone ecosystem now counts about six hundred grizzlies, and the Glacier ecosystem also totals about six hundred, with about another hundred bears scattered throughout the West in isolated pockets, such as Idaho's Selkirk Mountains and the Cabinet–Yaak area of Montana and Idaho. (Beyond the American West, in Canada and Alaska, there's still a healthy population total of about forty thousand grizzlies.)

True, grizzly numbers in the West are still a far cry from the estimated fifty thousand that once roamed the region, but the great bear is slowly spreading beyond the current paltry 2 percent of its historic habitat. In recent years, a few bears have moved into the northern Cascade Mountains in Washington state, and considering the vast tracts of prime bear habitat in Oregon and Colorado, it's only a matter of time before the tracks of the great bear are once again found in those states. In addition, grizzlies have expanded their ranges in Idaho, Montana, and Wyoming.

But the best news may be the plan proposed by the U.S. Fish and Wildlife Service to reintroduce the grizzly to the Bitterroot Mountains, which form the two-hundred-mile-long boundary between Idaho and Montana. This vast tract of wilderness, comprising more than six thousand square miles, encompasses the Selway–Bitterroot Wilderness Area and the Frank Church–River of No Return Wilderness Area. There are millions of acres of prime grizzly habitat in this remote land.

The plan calls for the release of five grizzly bears in the area each year for six years, with the sixth group to be released in 2007. They would come from Canada, interior Alaska, Yellowstone National Park, or the northern Rockies. No problem bears associated with run-ins with humans or livestock would be used. It would take about fifty years for full recovery, but eventually there would be about three hundred grizzlies in the Bitterroots.

Considering the tremendous pressure the bear is experiencing from encroachment of civilization on its habitat in the Glacier and Yellowstone ecosystems, the Bitterroot plan is a chance to ensure a healthy grizzly population for future generations. But it has encountered potential problems.

Human development right up to the boundaries of the Bitterroot Wilderness in Montana is sure to lure some bears down to the many old apple orchards in the heavily populated valley. And in Idaho, Governor Dirk Kempthorne penned an alarmist statement: "I oppose bringing these massive, flesh-eating carnivores into Idaho. This is perhaps the first federal land management action in history likely to result in injury or death to members of the public."

Kempthorne makes it sound like the bears will turn into man-eaters upon release. It's a scare tactic used by many individuals and special interest groups who want the Bitterroots for their own use. Unfortunately, it has worked. The federal government, bowing to political pressure, has put a hold on the Bitterroot grizzly reintroduction plan.

■ ■ ■

Any bear manager will tell you that habitat is the key to the grizzly's survival—for the present population and for future expansion. But as the grizzly inches back into its historic haunts, it finds itself a trespasser infringing upon the property and lifestyles of the New West's residents: open-range cattle and sheep ranchers, lodge and ski resort operators, homeowners in rural subdivisions, and commercial loggers and miners.

The result is the same management problem that has plagued wildlife biologists since day one: grizzly bears and people don't mix well. It remains a sobering fact that grizzlies occasionally attack and injure or kill humans, as the stories in this book demonstrate. The mix of bears and people also can end with a dead bear. In the year 2000, twenty grizzly bears were killed, legally or otherwise, by humans in the Glacier ecosystem, the most in fifteen years.

Chris Servheen, grizzly bear recovery coordinator for the U.S. Fish and Wildlife Service, was quoted in the *Missoulian* as saying, "The majority of our dead bears now occur where we have people building and developing private land in grizzly habitat. These private lands are the source of more than 60 percent of the human–bear conflicts. Very few bears die on public land. Most die on private land, and the source is usually people feeding wild animals or leaving garbage or dog food out.

"These new residents who move to Montana want a piece of the wilderness and build a big house, complete with bird feeder in the backyard and a tub-sized deer feeder out front. When you do that in bear country, you end up with grizzlies in your front and back yards."

Though the grizzly as an individual remains a powerful force in nature, the species as a whole is extremely sensitive to disruptions in its population density. Studies of isolated grizzly populations suggest that when the number falls below fifty bears, that particular bear enclave is at risk of disappearing.

One reason is that grizzlies require a vast range to find enough food to survive, and they probably can't always locate each other to mate. Compounding this predicament is the grizzly's austere reproductive cycle. A female must be five years old before she is biologically ready to reproduce, and only once every three years thereafter will she mate. Even then, her cubs have less than a 50 percent chance of surviving to maturity. With those numbers, it's easy to see how a few excess killings can greatly harm, and in some cases eliminate, a small grizzly population.

The question, then, is the definition of "excess killings." When does a grizzly killing become excessive? Are they all excessive, as some bear conservationists contend? Or is there such a thing as "normal" bear mortality?

In those fringe areas where bear and human coexist in an uneasy truce, most bear biologists agree that there will be a certain amount of bear mortality due to the animal's proximity to civilization. A study of the Yellowstone ecosystem found that 64 percent of all grizzly deaths occurred within a mile and a half of roads and three miles of major developments.

Bears also get run over by trains and hit by cars—the usual mishaps that occur with other wildlife species, such as deer and elk, that live near the fringes of civilization. Added to these deaths is the natural mortality among grizzlies from fights, starvation, natural accidents, and disease. But in spite of this yearly death toll, the great bear has held its own and is slowly increasing in some areas.

■ ■ ■

It's an unfortunate fact that bears must sometimes be removed from a particular ecosystem because they have become habituated and have lost their natural fear of humans. Given its aggressive, opportunistic nature, a habituated grizzly bear has the potential to pose a serious threat to property or human life. Habituated bears were responsible for the deaths, related earlier in this book, of Craig Dahl, Bill Tesinsky, and Michio Hoshino; these were bears that had lost their natural fear of people.

Most bear habituation occurs when humans fail, through ignorance or neglect, to take simple precautions in bear country. A good example is the backyard bird feeder. Wildlife managers constantly preach the hazards of placing out high-protein birdseed in bear country, yet the average rural resident remains blissfully ignorant, or indifferent, to its damaging effects as a habituator of bears.

Birdseed even has the potential to stifle a promising bear population. In 2000, wildlife biologists monitoring a female grizzly in Montana were excited when the bear moved from its northern Continental Divide home into the Selkirk Mountains of northern Idaho. In the twenty-five years since grizzly bears were given protection under the Endangered Species Act, it was the first time a female had moved from Montana into Idaho's Selkirks.

But the two-year-old female started frequenting backyard bird feeders north of Bonners Ferry, Idaho. Disconsolate biologists reluctantly trapped the bear and relocated her back to Montana—all because of a bird feeder in bear country.

Once a bear eats human food, it is very difficult to break the bear from associating people with a food reward. Some biologists claim it's just about impossible. Expensive bear management programs, such as relocating problem bears, have proven largely ineffective. The relocated bear often hurries back to its former haunt or goes elsewhere to find trouble.

A new bear management technique, which uses aversive conditioning, has shown tremendous potential for rehabilitating problem bears. Carrie Hunt, who helped develop bear pepper spray with Chuck Jonkel, has created a bear-dog program that works to set boundaries for problem bears. A bear that steps over the line from wild to habituated is set upon by Hunt and her Karelian bear dogs. The big, powerful dogs harass the bear intensely while Hunt and her associates sting the bear's rump with rubber bullets.

Bears are intelligent animals and quick learners, and the bear-dog technique sets an imaginary boundary that tells them they are going to experience pain and harassment if they go near a human dwelling again. Hunt follows up each bear-dog treatment with an intense door-to-door campaign to educate local residents of proper food and activity management in bear country.

So far, Hunt's bear-dog treatment has been very successful. It has been necessary to relocate only one bear out of the two hundred habituated bears she has conditioned with her Karelian bear dogs. That bear's name was Stahr, a female grizzly with two cubs. Back in 1997, Stahr had begun feeding on bait left out by a wildlife photographer. When that ended, she began pilfering dog food, garbage, and birdseed left out by residents along the North Fork Flathead River west of Glacier. Soon the emboldened bear was breaking down doors and smashing windows to get at the easy human food.

Hunt and fellow bear biologist Tim Manley worked Stahr hard, sending her fleeing back to the wilderness amidst a barrage of rubber bullets and Karelian bear dogs nipping at her rump. In the meantime, residents of that area were urged to remove all food attractants that might tempt the bear to return. The treatment seemed to work. Stahr stayed clear of human developments for a year and a half.

"We thought our treatment was a huge success," Hunt said in a *Missoulian* interview. "We thought we had her turned around. We thought we were going to show that even a bear that had been tearing down doors could be turned around."

But then the bear-dog funding dried up. And sloppy food handling by local residents once again lured Stahr back to the North Fork area. Unknown to Manley or Hunt, Stahr again began nosing around residences in the North Fork area. People saw her, watched her, and were sometimes entertained by her as she fed on dog food, livestock feed, and food left for her in backyards. They may as well have fed her poison. The final straw was a midnight raid by Stahr at the Home Ranch Store, where she literally peeled the storefront siding away to gain access to the food inside.

The young sow had become a hopelessly habituated bear. "Before we live-trapped her," Hunt said, "we gave her a few last days of freedom to roam, and we followed her. It was a real eye-opener. She told us a story of easy food. She took us to bird feeders, horse feed, human food. She took us to people who just shrugged and said, 'Yep, she's been around for quite a while.' Obviously, people ignored our instructions on how to live safely in bear country." Stahr and her cubs were sent off to a research facility in Washington state.

■ ■ ■

It doesn't take an expert with a Ph.D. in wildlife biology to tell us that ignorance is the real enemy of the grizzly bear. Ignorance among farmers and ranchers in the early 1900s about the low risk of bear predation on their livestock was the catalyst that permitted the slaughter of the grizzly bear in the continental United States.

The ignorance continues today. Ignorance of bear behavior and basic bear-avoidance procedures results in untold numbers of hikers blithely striding toward potential disaster in our national parks. It was ignorance of proper food storage practices in bear country that doomed Stahr and her cubs to a steel cage.

Education is the antithesis of ignorance. Where ignorance of the propensity for a startled grizzly to charge sends a hiker, head down and silent, padding along a brushy trail, education reminds that same hiker to always be bear aware and to make plenty of noise before entering any area with limited sight distance. Where ignorance of the benefits of carrying bear spray places both human and bear at risk, education sends that hiker along the trail with a can of EPA-registered bear spray on his or her belt, just in case the unthinkable occurs.

And with the rapid encroachment of civilization upon remaining grizzly habitat, education in proper behavior when hiking or living in bear country becomes the key to the great bear's survival. High-profile people and organizations are needed to preach sound management practices to help the average citizen better understand the bear and avoid trouble in bear country.

The Center for Wildlife Information, in Missoula, accomplishes this task by working with state, federal, and private agencies to produce wildlife stewardship programs for the public on how to camp, hike, and photograph in the wild without danger to human or animal.

The official spokesman for the Center for Wildlife Information, retired General Norman Schwarzkopf, is quoted in the center's brochure: "During my years with the U.S. Army, I traveled all over the world and learned we have something special in North America few other areas have: pristine wildlands and abundant wildlife. Animals, especially bears, need space just like you and me. Learning to enjoy wildlife from a responsible distance will help ensure that wildlife thrives for years to come. Take the time to learn how to enjoy animals without endangering them or you."

To those wise words from a true American hero, every beleaguered wildlife manager breathes a collective "Amen!"

For More Information

BOOKS

Alaska Bear Tales and *More Alaska Bear Tales*, by Larry Kaniut. Alaska Northwest Books. 1-800-452-3032; www.gacpc.com.

Bear Attacks: The Deadly Truth, by James Gary Shelton. Pallister Publishing. 1-800-336-3137.

Bear Attacks: Their Causes and Avoidance, by Stephen Herrero. The Lyons Press. 1-888-249-7586; www.globepequot.com.

Bear vs. Man, by Brad Garfield. Willow Creek Press. 1-800-850-9453; www.willowcreekpress.com.

Chocolate Legs, by Roland Check. Skyline Publishing. 1-800-821-6784.

Great Montana Bear Stories, by Ben Long. Riverbend Publishing. 1-866-787-2363; www.riverbendpublishing.com.

Grizzly Years, by Doug Peacock. Henry Holt. 1-888-330-8477; www.henryholt.com.

Self Defense for Nature Lovers, by Mike Lapinski. Stoneydale Press. 1-800-735-7006; www.stoneydale.com.

VIDEOS

Bear Attacks: Avoidance, Biology, Bear Spray, written, filmed, and produced by Mike Lapinski. Stoney-Wolf Productions. 1-800-237-7583; www.stoneywolf.net.

Grisan, Stoney-Wolf Productions. 1-800-237-7583; www.stoney-wolf.net.

ORGANIZATIONS

Center for Wildlife Information, P.O. Box 8289, Missoula, MT 59807. 1-406-523-7750; www.marsweb.com/~rattlesnake.

The Great Bear Foundation, P.O. Box 9383, Missoula, MT 59807. 1-406-829-9378; www.greatbear.org.

About the Author

Mike Lapinski resides in Superior, Montana, where he lives in harmony with bears and his wife, Aggie. He often writes about bears when he's not hiking the Loop Trail in his beloved Glacier National Park and viewing the great bears from a safe distance.

Lapinski is an outdoors writer whose books include *The Elk Mystique* and *Self Defense for Nature Lovers*. His writing has appeared in numerous magazines, including *Outdoor Life, Sports Afield,* and *Field & Stream*. He speaks frequently to audiences throughout the West on the subject of keeping safe in the wild.

CPSIA information can be obtained
at www.ICGtesting.com
Printed in the USA
BVOW08s0918260118
506043BV00001B/1/P